THE BUOY

PROJECTS

A Story of Breast Cancer, Bucket-Lists,
Life Lessons, Facebook and Love

Lorna J. Brunelle

authorHOUSE®

AuthorHouse™
1663 Liberty Drive
Bloomington, IN 47403
www.authorhouse.com
Phone: 1 (800) 839-8640

Published by AuthorHouse   06/23/2016

ISBN: 978-1-5246-0046-4 (sc)
ISBN: 978-1-5246-0045-7 (e)

Library of Congress Control Number: 2016905177

Print information available on the last page.

Any people depicted in stock imagery provided by Thinkstock are models, and such images are being used for illustrative purposes only. Certain stock imagery © Thinkstock.

This book is printed on acid-free paper.

Because of the dynamic nature of the Internet, any web addresses or links contained in this book may have changed since publication and may no longer be valid. The views expressed in this work are solely those of the author and do not necessarily reflect the views of the publisher, and the publisher hereby disclaims any responsibility for them.

There is no right or wrong way to deal with a diagnosis of incurable disease whether that's cancer or any other untreatable condition. Any book that tells you there is a formula for successfully handling dying and death is either over-simplifying or over-promising but some books can give you some valuable ideas, suggestions and shared experience to help you through difficult times. I believe this is one of those books.

Diagnosis doesn't come with a downloadable guide, a tick-list or a computer tracker. Everybody who hears that they can't be cured is a first-timer, a new member of the terminal club. Each will find their own way to handle their situation and to use the time that's left. Cancer and other terminal diseases don't only affect the patient; they have drastic impact on everyone around the patient too. Whether you are the person with the terminal diagnosis or you're the partner, child, parent, friend or colleague of somebody facing life's biggest challenge, this book offers valuable tools to help with that challenge.

Why do I say this? Because this book doesn't claim to get everything right. It's just the story of one woman and how she did her utmost to live her life to the fullest and to prepare her family and friends for the time when she would no longer be around. Take from this book what you want and put aside what you doesn't feel right for you. We are all different. Look for the aspects of her 'bucket list' approach that work for you and think about giving some of them a go.

Wanda Stairs Howard was many things to many people but first and foremost, she was a mother, grandmother and wife. Her daughter Lorna's book is an account of how Wanda took what was left of her life and squeezed it until the pips squeaked, how she and her tireless 'Team Wanda' celebrated her life whilst she was still living it, and how eventually they set her free for the ultimate journey.

This book was written because so many people responded so strongly to her story as it played out through the medium of Facebook and many of those people asked Lorna to put her mother's story into print so that she could inspire others who weren't lucky enough to know her personally. By the end of the book, I hope that readers will feel like they knew Wanda and that many will take comfort and inspiration from her life and death.

~Barbara Lunnon, Cancer advocate

Thank you

*This book would not have been possible without the unending support of family, friends and everyone who loved Wanda. Like a buoy, **Team Wanda** elevated my mother and kept her afloat while she navigated her voyage from earth to heaven. **Roger** ~ Thank you for being the captain of our ship. Your love anchors me. **Elizabeth, Tahlia, Doug, Paige, Tyler, Taylor, Trey and Linda** ~ You are the best deckhands a crew could ask for. Even during the roughest seas, humor sustained us until the storm passed. **Mason** ~ You are our lighthouse. Thank you for making every day brighter. **Maureen** ~ You are the best stewardess on the sea. Thank you for holding down the ship. **Jennifer** ~ Like a figurehead on the prow of a ship's bow, you kept me pointed in the right direction. **Barbara** ~ You are one heck of a first mate. Thank you for keeping my head above the water when the writing felt like a rogue wave. **Danny and Jane** ~ Thanks for being my dinghy. Thanks to you, we smoothly sailed to the early morning appointments. **Lisa Buzzell- Curley / Angels in America** ~ You are the best harbormaster! You did an epic job patrolling for buoys. **Mermaids and dolphins** ~ You know who you are. Thank you for being gorgeous and for swimming by my side until I was able to come up to the surface for air. I love you all.*

Cover Design / Book Jacket: Joshua Narciso

*Some names have been changed to protect the privacy of people in this story.

This book is in celebration of my mother
Wanda Stairs Howard

What is done in love is done well. ~Vincent van Gogh

Contents

Foreword

IN THE SUMMER OF 1970 A teenage girl named Wanda sat in a room with her parents and a nun. She was Vice President of her class, had excellent grades, sang in the Glee Choir, and loved English and art class. She also loved a boy. Through this love a baby was conceived.

Wanda thought the purpose of the meeting was to decide where she was going to live for the duration of her pregnancy. She was familiar with Catholic homes for girls who had fallen from grace. She thought girls were allowed to work at these homes in exchange for a roof over their heads, a chance to spare their families the humiliation of a pregnancy out of wedlock, and above all, to avoid the sin of abortion.

Minutes into the meeting it became evident that once the baby was born, Wanda would be expected to leave the home. The infant, however, would be expected to remain with the nuns. The nuns would find a family to adopt the child.

This plan was crystal clear to Wanda's mother. Her father was a little more foggy on the protocol. He assumed his daughter would live with the nuns in the home, give birth, find a job (or a boy who would marry her) and adapt to motherhood. When he asked the nun if Wanda would have the option of keeping her child at the end of the stay, the answer was no.

Giving up her baby was never part of Wanda's plan. Overcome with panic, she looked at her father wondering if he would let her keep her child. After a long silence, Wanda's dad spelled out her options.

Her first option was to stay with the nuns through February when the baby was born. After which, she would leave the baby, return to finish school, and have her whole life ahead of her.

Her second option was to drop out of school, raise a child as an unwed mother, sacrifice her reputation, her freedom, and the pursuit of art, music, and education. Her future would be filled with struggle. The decision was hers to make. She would have their love and support either way.

Wanda gave birth to me on February 6, 1971. She named me after her best friend Lorna. A man who wasn't my biological father (but that's another story entirely) married her and gave both of us his last name. A few years later, they conceived my sister Elizabeth whom we call Liz. Years later, mum remarried and my sister Tahlia was born.

Against all odds, Wanda built a beautiful life on a foundation of family. She spent her fifty-nine years on earth building a legacy of love. As she faced death during her final ten months, she taught thousands of people how to live and love. Many of these people asked us to share her journey with you and that's why her story became this book. This is a story about a remarkable woman who taught everyone who knew her how to live while she learned how to die, one bucket list item, miracle, and life lesson at a time.

Each chapter will end with a Facebook post from Wanda's wall. Selected to portray her personality, they may not always pertain to events chronicled in the preceding chapter.

We have two lives, and the second begins when we realize we only have one. - **Confucius**

1

Don't Forget Tomato Paste

HE SOUND OF WANDA POUNDING CHICKEN cutlets in her kitchen sent a Morse code alert to the neighborhood that a delicious meal was up ahead. When the hammering stopped, my sisters and I stood tableside helping her bathe each cutlet in an egg wash. From there we would coat them in a mixture of breadcrumbs and cheese.

The smell of the hot oil frying each cutlet into a crispy masterpiece made our bellies rumble. Wearing an outfit and hairstyle from the latest fashion, perfectly applied makeup and gold hoop earrings, Wanda would turn the cutlets and say, "I make mine paper thin so they fry fast. You have to watch them every second so they won't burn. It is a lot of extra work to get them this thin, but it is worth it." She would stop to puff her cigarette in between sentences.

After a brief rest on top of paper towels, the mouthwatering cutlets were sprinkled with salt and piled high on top of plates. I remember eye balling the mountains of culinary perfection awaiting the moment when mum would allow us to sample the labor of her love. In our home food and love went together like spaghetti and meatballs. Everyone was welcome around Wanda's table.

My favorite meal was her beef braciole. I remember standing on a stool near the counter watching mum cut and pound the flank steak. After placing stuffing (usually a sautéed onion, cheese and breadcrumb mixture) in the middle of the steak, she would roll each section of the stuffed steak.

From there, she would wrap individual steak servings in white kitchen twine. My job was to place my finger on top of the steak as she tied strong knots. "The rope holds the steak together when we fry it in the pan. We don't want the stuffing to fall out before we put the meat in the sauce," she'd say as I carefully held my finger in place. "You're doing such a good job. You're going to be a great cook when you grow up."

Once all of the meat was seared, she would begin her sauce. Shortly after we heard the sizzle from the onions diving into the extra virgin olive oil, she'd say, "You have to wait for the onions to become see-through before you add your tomato paste. This is very important. You can't rush the sauce."

Once the sautéed onions became translucent, Wanda would add tomato paste. "Not everyone starts their sauce off with tomato paste. I use it because I like a thicker sauce." She would remove the pot from the stove and hold the handles so I could look inside to see the process.

"When I took the paste out of the can it was bright red. See how it is becoming darker now like almost a maroon color? This means the paste has had enough time in the oil with the onions. Now we are ready to add our other ingredients. If you want a delicious and thick sauce don't forget tomato paste."

As much as Wanda loved to cook, she loved to sing. She had a face and figure that was made for the stage and a voice that was made for the radio. The daughter of a Sicilian mother and Native American father, her striking beauty and natural talent landed her jobs as a singer in nightclubs.

Growing up, there was always music playing in our home. Some days she would belt out Cher in the kitchen. Other days she would sing Diana Ross solos into a hairbrush as she danced around with us in the parlor. In the dining room she would wail Tom Jones and Leslie Gore ballads as we set the table. We would sit audience in her bedroom as she rehearsed the Dorothy Moore version of "Misty Blue." I was never able to differentiate her voice from the album playing in the background.

Country music had yet to take the east coast by storm, but Wanda was known to sing Patsy Cline's "Crazy", Tammy Wynette's "Stand By Your Man" and Dolly Parton's "Jolene" every time they were featured on the variety TV shows she watched. Although she was a child of the Beatles, her adult solo repertoire consisted mostly of torch songs. She liked the cathartic power of songs about hardship or heartbreak.

Despite a rocky history of romance, Wanda never gave up on her fairytale. Her happily ever after was about motherhood not Prince Charming. The men in her life would come and go, but her children were hers forever. According to mum, the chance to love us and be loved by us was all she ever needed.

When my sisters gave birth to their children, Wanda experienced a different kind of love. Her grandchildren Paige, Tyler, Taylor and Trey were born between 1992 and 2004. Her enthusiasm for being a grandmother was endless. The kids were the first thing she thought of when she woke up in the morning and the last thing she thought of when she went to bed at night.

She was glad she had her children when she was young. As a young grandmother she had the energy to fully submerge herself in the daily routine of the grandkids. During this exciting time, she married a good man named Doug. They stayed together for the rest of her life.

In the mix of all of these new beginnings, a breast cancer diagnosis tried to slow Wanda down. With our loving family at her side, she fought and triumphed over the disease in 2009. Shortly after, she welcomed a puppy named Emma Mae to our family and continued soaking in the privilege of being a doggy-mom as well as grandmother. Five years after her first diagnosis, the breast cancer metastasized. This is when the love Wanda had spent her entire life fostering shone its purest beauty.

<u>Wanda Stairs Howard</u> <u>August 26, 2013</u>

Remember the memories that you've made in life, think of them often, that way you get to enjoy the experiences more than just once!

2

Be True to Yourself

WANDA WAS A TRAILBLAZER. DURING A time when society frowned on young girls having children out of wedlock, she had a baby. Later in life, she married a black man when bi-racial marriages in the United States were socially scandalous. As the mother of a mixed race child (my sister Tahlia) Wanda proudly faced discrimination and bigotry in the name of love and the right to love. She obtained her G.E.D. decades after she was supposed to have graduated from high school and went on to graduate from Paralegal School. She used her creativity to work at a high paying job in newspaper advertising.

In search of something more rewarding, she left this lucrative job and became a Certified Nursing Assistant. She shared her compassion and empathy as a hospice worker for patients with cancer and AIDS. This was during a time when the world was paralyzed with fear at the very mention of HIV.

Her fearless and compassionate spirit brought her to the bedside of the sick and dying. She incorporated her love of fashion and beauty with the way she cared for each person. Her work tool box included nail polish, curlers, combs, brushes, and scented hand cream. For hours she would sit with her beloved hospice friends, massaging their hands and feet, setting their hair, and painting their nails. She helped them preserve grace, beauty, and dignity in their deaths.

During our childhood mum was the neighborhood barber, hair stylist, and beautician. Without any formal training she would help those who couldn't afford a cut, color, or style in a salon. She loved visiting the wholesale beauty shops and stocking up on supplies to help beautify her friends. I loved watching her make people look and feel pretty in our home. Her giving heart instilled confidence in everyone.

While people were complaining about the homeless population in Boston, Wanda was giving money, food, and cigarettes to those wrapped in blankets on the side of the road. As a tireless advocate for the downtrodden, she loved her time as a volunteer for Catholic Charities. No matter what society deemed right or wrong, Wanda remained true to herself.

Wanda never forgot how difficult it was to raise three girls with very little financial and emotional support. There were many times when I watched mum take the final twenty dollars out of her pocketbook and hand it to someone who needed formula and diapers for their baby. With very little money in her checking account, she would go without for the rest of the week until her next check was cashed. If she realized someone had fallen on hard times, she would leave a shopping bag filled with food or gently used clothing at their door.

Even when she had breast cancer, Wanda insisted on taking care of the people around her. She supplied everyone in her chemo center (nurses and patients) with gifts and food at each chemo session. Some days she would pass out religious medals or rosary beads. Other days she would share magazines or homemade sesame cookies or strawberry shortcake.

Wanda's love of food was not minimized during chemo. To the contrary, the steroids in her chemo drip sent her appetite into overdrive. We planned daily adventures around food. Champagne with strawberries, blueberries with lemon curd, oranges with cream, and mocha with raspberries were a few of the reasons why we piled into my Jeep one afternoon.

One hundred and thirty-five feet above the ocean, we crossed the Cape Cod Canal in search of the latest trendy, foodie craze - gourmet cupcakes. With mum by my side and my friend Mo seated behind her, we were on a cupcake mission. We welcomed any excuse to break away from the ordinary. Lumpectomies, double mastectomies, chemo, radiation, reconstruction, and breast cancer had become our ordinary. Mum and Mo had breast cancer surgery one business day apart during the late spring of 2009.

Wanda spent that summer indulging in overpriced pastries and planning adventures. The anticipation of each new outing served as a buffer to the chemo center and exam rooms. She buried her mind in research. Dog-earing the pages of the lists of Boston Magazine Zagat-rated restaurants and five-star hotels became our sport. Hotels with luxurious spas that were way out of our price range were earmarked first.

Oprah visited the Cape that summer to attend the funeral of Eunice Kennedy Shriver. The local papers quoted her praising a local spot in Centerville for having the best homemade pies. The day the story broke we gassed up the Jeep and headed back over the bridge - great pie has special powers. A part of me believes delicious pie can win a street fight with cancer.

Neither the cupcakes nor the pies were especially 'drop-your-fork' fabulous, but spontaneity made us feel in control of our happiness. The ability to remain impulsive during a time when most everything was scheduled and played out to somebody else's agenda was more delicious than any butter and sugar frosting.

This was mum's first time at the breast cancer and cupcakes rodeo. She only went to her primary care physician seeking help for her debilitating hot flashes. Hormone replacement therapy (HRT) was rumored to be the surefire cure. A five-year lapse in time between mammograms had crept up on mum. To be safe, her doctor ordered a mammogram before prescribing the HRT.

The images showed a large mass and a biopsy determined it was cancer. The surgeries, pathology reports, and lymph node involvement confirmed the advanced staging of her disease. To be precise, she had Stage 3, Estrogen-based breast cancer. Of the seventeen lymph nodes removed, eight of them were cancerous.

Wanda's surgery was in Boston, about 45 miles away from home. Traffic is a beast in our tiny Bay State, so we planned our hotel trips around follow-up visits with mum's rock star surgeon. The Best of the Best, this doctor's patients included a long list of high profile women including Elizabeth Edwards and Teresa Heinz-Kerry.

By the third week of August, Wanda was completely bald from chemo. She looked so stunning in her scarves and wigs that a staff member of the Park Plaza Hotel couldn't resist mum's wide-eyed request to tour the Presidential Suite during our stay there. With the pride of a true daughter of Massachusetts and her love of all things 'Camelot' Wanda glowed with pleasure as she told me "John F. Kennedy slept here."

The next day the media announced the death of Senator Edward (Ted) Kennedy. Cancer has a way of leveling social status and is no respecter or wealth or position. During her fight with cancer, mum often referred to "Ted's cancer" as if they had sat side by side sharing crackers in the same chemo center. The camaraderie between cancer patients is both beautiful and heartbreaking.

Mum and I went to the Basilica of Our Lady of Perpetual Help in a section of Boston named Mission Hill. We lit candles and prayed for Ted the day before his funeral. President Barack Obama was scheduled to attend the service. News reporters lined the streets.

A reporter approached Wanda and asked if she wanted to share a few words about the passing of the Senator. Looking flawless in her perfectly applied makeup and scarf, mum offered raw words about life, love, and cancer.

When the camera stopped, she turned to me and said, "All of the money and power in the world can't save us once it is our time to go. This is why we have to plan adventures and make the most out of every single day. This is why we have to celebrate all of the moments in life and have to have fun. We never know when the end will come."

Wanda Stairs Howard February 13, 2

I love asking little kids what they want to be wh
up . . . cause, you know . . . I'm still looking

3

Experience the Best of the Best

As A FAMILY WE SPENT THE next five years after her diagnosis making a strong effort to honor mum's request for more fun. We'd load up the grandchildren and visit the coast of New Hampshire and Cape Cod. Weekends involved sleepovers with the grandkids at mum's house in Buzzards Bay, Massachusetts. These getaways always involved some form of arts and crafts, cooking, reading, eating, yard work, walking the canal, shopping, or preparing projects for school. The weekends with the grandkids mirrored the weekends of my childhood. Wanda always sought fun.

We continued scouting the 'Best of Boston' section of local magazines. We prided ourselves in finding the best cheeseburger, the best soul food, the best cannoli, and the best breakfast. We saw the best of the best movies, a few of which we walked out of once we realized the critics weren't always right. Life really is too short for bad movies.

We walked through bookstores picking up two copies so that we could read them in parallel. Our family watched the same TV shows so we could stay up late gossiping about the players in each storyline.

We poked through shops smelling soap and candles. We never missed a chance to attend birthday parties, holidays, and special occasions.

Life and work kept moving on and about a year into mum's recovery I expanded my performing arts school business by opening a small theatre. Our entire family came together and worked on the project. Mum left her creative mark on nearly every wall of the 11,000 square foot space. Several comedy headliners played at the theatre. Each season there was a terrific line up of great shows and talented artists. As a family, we spent a lot of time seeing shows, concerts, and plays together at the theatre.

The performing arts are part of our family DNA. While Wanda was singing at local night clubs around Boston, her brother was the lead singer in a band. Their grandmother from Sicily had a beautiful voice for opera. During the early 90's mum enjoyed working as a karaoke disc jockey on weekends. If you closed your eyes you would have thought Patsy Cline or Cher had stepped up to the mic; mum's voice was that good.

Singing brought mum a lot of joy and even may have extended her life. In the summer of 2013, my sisters took mum to a local Chinese restaurant known for their karaoke lounge. Having not sung in a while, mum was disappointed in her vocal quality. This was the first time I remember hearing her say she had a hard time catching her breath. She assumed the chest and neck radiation (following her chemo) must have altered her voice.

After the karaoke night we began noticing a change in her breathing. For a few weeks mum sounded like she had developed a summer cold. In addition to her breathing issues, she was often tired and needed to nap. She visited her doctor and asked for a chest X-ray. They listened to her lungs, which sounded clear so the request for the X-ray was ignored.

I drove her to a local pulmonary specialist to rule out chronic obstructive pulmonary disease (COPD) or advanced emphysema. She was a lifelong smoker and was never in denial about the risks associated with smoking.

Without even sending for an X-ray, the specialist recommended immediate home oxygen for sleeping. He also ordered a test that involved her walking around a track while being hooked up to some type of device. This test was scheduled a month away. The patient advocate in me came out at the reception area once I heard that the reason why we had to wait a month for the test was that the specialist was going on vacation.

The next day mum had a complete meltdown over the idea of adding oxygen tanks to her life without even knowing what caused the change in her lungs. As she cried on the phone to me, I heard how desperately she struggled for air. She sounded as if she were drowning. As soon as we hung up I called my sisters and within minutes we had a plan. We were taking mum to the ER in Boston.

The optimist in me thought she needed an antibiotic for pneumonia. The realist in me thought there was a possibility her cancer had decided to spend another summer with us. I called her surgeon and oncologist to let them know we were on our way. Nurses from both of their offices agreed it was the best course of action. There was no reason to mess around with local hospitals and doctors when the best doctors in the world were at our fingertips in Boston. In the spirit of the best of the best, we headed to the city.

A Few of Wanda's Foodie Favorites. The Best of the Best.
Lobster Pie - The Causeway, Gloucester, Massachusetts
Breakfast- Uncommon Grounds, Watertown, Massachusetts
Comfort Food - The Common Man, Portsmouth, New Hampshire
Greek Food - Desfina, Cambridge, Massachusetts
Surf and Turf- The Capital Grill, Boston, Massachusetts
Mongolian Hot Pot- Little Lamb, Boston, Massachusetts
Soul Food- The Coast Cafe, Cambridge, Massachusetts
Deli- S & S Restaurant, Cambridge, Massachusetts
Iced Coffee- Mirasol's Cafe, Dartmouth, Massachusetts
Pastry- Antoine's Pastry Shop, Newton, Massachusetts
Sandwich- Tutto Italiano, Lakeville, Massachusetts
Chinese - Orchid of Hawaii, Lakeville, Massachusetts
Cannoli- TIE: Antonio's, Boston, Massachusetts and
Modern Pastry, North End, Massachusetts
Armenian Food- The Armenian Market, Watertown, Massachusetts

Buffet- TIE: The Nordic Lodge, Charlestown, Rhode
Island and The Brazilian Grill, Hyannis, Massachusetts
Fried Zucchini- Maggiano's, Boston, Massachusetts
Ice Cream- Emack and Bolio's, Boston, Massachusetts
Fried Clam Cakes - Betty Ann's, Buzzard's Bay, Massachusetts
Malasada- School Street Bakery, Taunton, Massachusetts

*Although we ate at *a lot* of Italian restaurants, mum was unable to rate a meatball, chicken cutlet or batch of sauce above her own.

<u>Wanda Stairs Howard</u> <u>April 26, 2013</u>

Anyone can make you happy by doing something special, but only someone special can make you happy without doing anything.

4

Laughter is Great Therapy

WANDA WAS GIVEN A CHEST X-RAY in the ER of the most famous hospital in Boston. Within five minutes we were looking at an image of her lungs which showed that 75% of her left lung was filled with fluid. She was, in effect, drowning. Before we had any time to process her condition, a team of doctors circled around us and explained what needed to be done. "We have to get this fluid out immediately. We have to go into the side of her rib cage and insert a rather large tube. This hose will drain the fluid. Unfortunately, this is going to hurt. There is no way around it. We have to move fast."

Five doctors began instructing me on how to help mum during the procedure. "You can hold this hand. You can help hold this part of her arm. You can hold this part of her shoulder. Whatever you do, you shouldn't move her once we get started. This entire procedure should take less than fifteen minutes. Please talk to your mother and remind her to keep breathing."

We had been in this boat before, mum and me. By boat I mean a situation involving something neither of us wanted to participate in. Four years prior in 2009, her surgeon wanted to rule out cancer in other areas of her body before cutting her open to remove her breast cancer. A CAT scan showed suspicious areas of concern in three other locations, her liver, her lung, and her chest. Mum had to go under for a thoracic biopsy, during which a "Pac-Man" type instrument grabs tiny pieces of chest cavity and lung tissue.

To look more closely at the liver mum needed an MRI scan. Several tablets of a sedative named Ativan, a facecloth folded over her eyes as a blindfold, and my promise never to leave her side were what it took to get our claustrophobic mother into the MRI scanner.

I asked if I could keep my hand on her head during the entire MRI. The staff agreed. I had no idea the machine was going to slide so far under and into the tube. My years of dance training paid off as I stretched my body across a pretty long distance to keep my hand on her head. Every time they asked my mother to breathe in and hold, I would sing the Alphabet Song or Twinkle, Twinkle Little Star. The songs were a way for her to gauge how long she needed to hold her breath. We repeated this game for the forty-five minute test.

The results were soon available. The spot on the liver was a hemangioma, a noncancerous mass in the liver that is made up of a tangle of blood vessels. The enlarged lymph nodes in the chest cavity and lung area were most likely caused by allergies, a cold, or being run down. We finally had the surgical green light for her lumpectomy. During the operation, her surgeon removed the lump from her breast and extracted seventeen lymph nodes. Eight of them contained cancer. The surgery was followed by 16 weeks of the strongest "sledgehammer" chemo, eight doses of chemo every other week, and 35 doses of radiation, five times a week over the course of seven weeks.

Before the surgery, mum asked if a mastectomy would enable her to skip chemo. I was there when the doctor said the following, "Wanda, you do not need a mastectomy. The location of the cancer is perfect for us to get to. You need chemo either way because of the lymph nodes." Mum and I had cancer in common. Four years before mum's diagnosis, I had thyroid cancer. This is the reason why I was usually the one to drive her to medical appointments, ask questions, and take notes. I am no longer intimidated by hospitals or people in white coats as people without a personal cancer experience may be.

Every year since her 2009 breast cancer surgery, mum had perfect mammograms. This apparent clean bill of health enabled us to let our guard down. Five years later, we sat vigil at mum's bedside in Boston petrified by her breathing setback wondering why there was so much fluid in mum's lung.

A catheter was inserted into mum's lung so fluid could continue to drain. Once the drain was dry, a really cool procedure was performed to seal the leaks. This involved injecting talc into the pleura of her lung and rotating her every fifteen minutes until the talc settled. Mum called this mad science "Fix-A-Flat."

Once the fluid subsided the team was able to lower the level of oxygen mum had piping into her nose and mouth. For nine days, we painstakingly waited for fluid samples, stains and tests to come back from pathology laboratory. During this time mum's husband Doug snuck Emma Mae into her hospital room. Part Bichon and part Shih Tzu, all ten pounds of fluffy therapy dog fit perfectly in one of mum's travel bags. We knew Emma Mae was the perfect medicine for mum.

On the morning of Wanda's 58th birthday, her oncologist confirmed that her cancer had metastasized to her lung and liver. A bone scan determined the disease was also on her tailbone, skull, and femur. Her cancer was terminal. The team spoke of ground-breaking treatments to prolong her life, but made it clear she would never be cured. Wanda could either get busy dying or get busy living. Our courageous and vibrant mother chose the latter.

Wanda smiled and laughed throughout her birthday celebration in the hospital. One would never suspect she had just learned that she was dying. Mum was awesome at smiling through pain. She always said laughter was her favorite therapy. Laughter was also a lot less selfish than tears.

The nurses threw a little party for her. She was showered in gifts, flowers and goodies. During the days leading up to mum's terminal diagnosis, we posted updates about her hospitalization on Facebook. The support mum received from friends dating back to grammar school via Facebook was astounding. Birthday messages, prayers, and posts of support blew up her phone.

Social networking is what lead to Wanda's greatest gift on that bittersweet birthday. Mum received an unexpected visit from her friend Linda. They were best friends for over 30 years, but for no serious reason they had fallen out of touch. Linda walked into the hospital and in a flash they picked up right where they had left off. The rekindling of this relationship would prove to be one of Wanda's great blessings.

Wanda concluded her birthday by taking the first medical step to prolong her life. Faslodex is an estrogen blocking medication that cuts off the food supply to her particular type of cancer. Estrogen had become cancer candy and we needed a strict diet, pronto. This medicine would block her estrogen and begin starving her cancer. This treatment was by no means a cure. This was a Band-Aid to buy us more time. Every decision Wanda made was for her children and grandchildren. We were her world. She spent her life building a family and wanted more time to help us embrace the inevitable.

The next day we packed up her hospital room and headed home. "Things are going to be different now," she said as we headed back to Buzzard's Bay. "I have a lot of living to do. We have to start planning." *Buckle up*, I thought, *Mum is about to take flight.*

Wanda Stairs Howard July 19, 2013 near Boston, MA

I am truly overwhelmed with the outpouring of love,
prayers and well wishes that I've received in the past week.
Words cannot express how it makes me feel. All of you
are amazing and I love each and every one of you.

5

Everyone Deserves an Entirely New Wardrobe

THE NEXT MORNING MUM SIPPED HER coffee in the kitchen as she scanned through Pinterest. She stopped on a photo that caught her eye. It was a beach themed kitchen with walls the color of sand, complemented by stark white bead board wainscoting and a shelf made from weathered white shutters. Starfish and sand dollars adorned the shelf. "I want this kitchen," she said, "I have always wanted a beachy kitchen. I spend a lot of time in this room. I'd really like to begin my bucket-listing in here."

This was the first time she mentioned bucket-listing. Fantastic at getting things done, mum began texting photos of her Pinterest kitchen to the entire family. Lucky for her, our crowd is comprised of carpenters, painters, and worker-bees. The renovation would be complete in two days. Lucky for us, this was a labor of love rather than money. Since all of the labor was free of charge, supplies and dollar store decorations were the only investment for the tiny beach chic kitchen.

From backsplash to wall color, wainscoting to window treatments, mum's beach kitchen was complete. Our husbands even built a little chair rail along the wall for her to place starfish and sand dollars. When I close my eyes I can see her clapping in gratitude, seated beside her favorite coffee cup. "I'm so blessed. Not everyone is handed this time to finish everything they want to do. This is a gift. Can you believe these curtains were only $1.49 at The Christmas Tree Shop?"

We spent a lot of time strolling around looking for perfect trinkets for her new cove. Mum had a flair for design and style. She took pride in her ability to make things beautiful. By things I mean just about everything: food, gardens, canvas, houses, life, and even people.

Not long after mum was discharged from the hospital, she began sorting through her things. Her first project was the photo albums. She went to a local craft store and bought each of us a container for photos. We sat on the floor of her cellar sorting through piles. When we were kids, mum loved showing us her photo albums. We would marvel at her style and beauty as the pages flipped through each decade. Cher inspired most of her wardrobe, makeup, accessories, and hairdos. Wanda was always the most beautiful girl in the room.

Mum began experiencing body pain. Sitting on the floor to sort through photos suddenly caused great pain in her joints. We called these episodes flare-ups. The tissues around her joints would swell, doubling in size. Her ankles, knees, and wrists were the most painful spots. For years mum's blood work presented several autoimmune disease antibodies, and although never firmly diagnosed, all signs pointed toward Lupus. We assumed her body was not amused about the starvation diet induced by the estrogen-blocking medication.

When the flare-ups occurred the only cure was a course of steroids. Eventually the flare-ups were lasting longer than the periods between them. Mum's oncologist prescribed daily steroids and at one point she was on an extremely high dose. With the high dose came high weight gain. Aside from pregnancy Wanda had never been round. At five feet tall, even the slightest weight gain makes a big difference. The extra pounds led us to yet another bucket list item, a whole new wardrobe.

We spent an entire weekend filling up her closet and dresser with hip new clothing to fit her hip new fuller figure. She said it was the first time in her life she had a new wardrobe. She had spent her life picking up pieces here and there as each season changed; a sweater on sale at

Marshalls one week, jeans on sale at Macy's the next, and a coat for more than half off at a consignment shop the following month.

Mum called me one morning and said, "Lorna, this is the first time in my life I have been able to open my closet without worrying about what I am going to wear. I have never set aside the time to put my needs first. I have always picked up one thing for myself and something for the kids or grandkids. Or one thing for myself and the rest of the money for the week went toward a bill. I mean, don't get me wrong, I love buying things for the kids, but women need to know how liberating this feels. Everyone needs to buy an entirely new wardrobe at least once before they die. I wish I learned this *before* I gained a ton of weight. I actually have something to look forward to every day when I wake up."

The sound of her words, laughter, and cigarette inhalation floated in perfect cadence through the phone line. This was the happiest I had heard her voice in a long while. I found myself struck by the paradox of her joyful spirit during the final phase of her life. "So, yeah, the bucket list, everyone needs to know how it feels to see a bunch of new things in their closet all at once. I mean it."

For the record, we are bargain queens. We shop with coupons, at outlet stores, and in the clearance section. We consider the hunt for the best deal more exciting than the purchase. You don't have to break the bank to spoil yourself. I ask that you honor this part of my mother's journey by buying yourself at least four new things to wear this week. Once, we found Wanda four articles of clothing for under $20.00.

Wanda's only expensive habits were her three loves: her grandchildren, cigarettes and coffee. Even after she learned of her terminal illness she kept on smoking. She tried the patch for a few weeks, but missed the art of smoking. I have never smoked a cigarette but respected her choice.

If anyone looked disapprovingly at her as she lit up she'd say, "Why should I stop now? I'm dying anyway, so really what difference does it make? Smoking makes me happy. Coffee makes me happy. I can't imagine one without the other. So there it is."

Mum would drink cups of coffee all day. She loved her Keurig coffee maker and had a taste for the most expensive K-cups. I loved hearing the story of her father, Ray, adding a little coffee to the milk in her baby bottle. I will never know if this story is true, but she glowed whenever she repeated it.

Keeping with the theme of her new body size, Wanda began posting positive affirmations about women loving their curves and embracing their size on her Facebook wall. This sort of thing was out of the ordinary for my mother. I spent the beginning of my life being very thin, but in my late twenties my thyroid tanked and I gained a remarkable amount of weight. As a plus-size woman in my forties I applauded my mother for preaching to ladies about size and worth through social networking. Wanda was brave and bold. God help the person who dared to write a comment about fat, heart health, or healthy weight under her posts.

Facebook and Instagram were extremely comforting to mum during this time. Thousands of people were able to hear her voice, support her and learn from her during the final phase of her life. A community of angels rallied around her. They even signed up to deliver her meals the first few weeks she came home from the hospital through a fabulous group called Take Them a Meal (www.takethemameal.com).

Wanda's internet family got her through many sleepless nights. Although many of her days were filled with adventure, many of mum's nights were filled with worry. These are the hours she shared with people her deepest thoughts about living and dying. This time at the computer sparked a new bucket list item.

<u>Wanda Stairs Howard</u> <u>October 31, 2013</u>

I get up every morning determined to both change the
world and have one hell of a good time. Sometimes this
makes planning my day difficult. E.B. White

6

Go After What You Want

WE'D START EACH DAY ON THE phone mapping out the plan for a day of fun. I'd dial mum's cell and she'd greet me with a robust, "Good morning!" One Saturday morning mum said, "You know what I have always wanted? An iPad. I literally would skip the mortgage payment to have an iPad. They are just too damn expensive for me to justify at full price, even though I am dying! (Insert ironic laughter) I wonder if we can find one used or on sale?"

Later that day our family headed out to Mirasol's Cafe in seaside town named Dartmouth for mum's favorite iced coffee, called a Chippi. The to-go cup for the regionally famous drink reads "Super Charged and Super Sexy Iced Coffee."

Since mum's diagnosis we had been rolling deep. Our average crew size for an iced coffee trip ranged between 6 and 12 people and required more than two vehicles in convoy. Everyone who loved mum became our family. We called ourselves Team Wanda. We even used a hashtag on our Instagram and Facebook posts, #TeamWanda. Together we made a conscious effort to celebrate the little moments (such as running out for a coffee) with big swagger. This support was yet another blessing brought to us by cancer. I encourage all of you to make memories by exploiting average opportunities.

As we sipped our drinks I couldn't stop thinking about the iPad. Mum had cancer in her tailbone. Sitting at the computer wasn't the most comfortable way for her to chat with her friends on Facebook. Surfing the internet on her phone was tricky because of the small screen size. Mum also had at least two or three treatments or doctors' appointments every month in Boston and long car rides in traffic were extremely uncomfortable on mum's lower back.

To ease the burden of each appointment we often spent the previous night in the city at an affordable hotel near the hospital. An iPad made sense for her new end-of-life life. In the true spirit of bucket-listing, we decided to venture to Best Buy to try our best to buy mum an affordable iPad. Luck and mum's bestie, Linda, were on our side. Ever the tech savvy pro, Linda worked her magic. In less than fifteen minutes Wanda was hooked up with an iPad.

She had craved this device for years but it took cancer to rest one in the palm of her hands. Herein lies yet another life lesson learned on mum's road to heaven...if you really, really want something and it is really, really within your reach to grab it- GRAB IT. If the thing you want is just outside of your reach, save up for it and then grab it or sell something you love less and grab it. Either way, grab it.

Wanda Stairs Howard August 27, 2013

Is painting a blue square in the backyard so
Google earth thinks I have a pool!

7

Become Queen for a Day

Mum's iPad was a total game changer. She spent hours on it at night communicating with people. Her online activity helped build the foundation for a community of support. Wanda was very open about her illness on Facebook. She answered questions, thanked people for their prayers, and posted daily about her final phase on earth.

People welcomed her honest and at times raw commentary on cancer. My heart was full of pride each time I'd read one of her posts about terminal illness. She always concluded her thought with something positive. She never once posted anything disrespectful about her disease. She frowned upon the idea of publically flipping cancer the bird for all the world to see on Facebook.

When mum gave up driving (because of the pain medication) her iPad was her link to the world. She passed the time checking in on her friends via the iPad during the hours we weren't there with her.

The iPad brought mum's love of the online game Candy Crush to a whole new level. "Now I have three addictions, coffee, cigarettes and Candy Crush," she'd say with a huge smile, hardly looking up from the screen. The cool thing about Candy Crush is that she was able to rely on friends for extra lives as she played.

The increased Facebook activity led to an unlimited amount of selfies. Before her illness mum thought selfies (photos of oneself or a small group of people standing together, taken with the lens button of a cell phone set on reverse) were for teenagers and conceited young adults. Wanda loathed the "kissing duck face" which dominated her newsfeed.

She referred to this lip squished expression as overplayed and unattractive. She even went so far as to inbox pretty girls who in mum's words "didn't look cute" posing with the duck face. She offered her advice, free of malice, hoping to help the girls capture prettier moments of their pretty faces.

Be that as it may, mum was seen posing with a kissing duck face or two alongside her young and stylish granddaughters, Paige and Taylor. As the traffic of mum's face increased on the internet she began thinking a lot about her hair. "You know what I'd love?" she said one morning. "An awesome hair style, a Newbury Street, high end salon hair style. A real sleek cut and color with a lot of depth."

Unlike her computer world iPad request, which I know nothing about, this request was right in my wheelhouse. I have never been one to splurge on my hair. Typically, I go to bed with wet hair once I have coated it with some type of anti-frizz product. For many years my mother cut and colored my hair, however through my profession I know a few Boston salon owners and more than a few stylists.

"I am pretty confident we can cross this off of your bucket list this week," I said. "Let me make some calls." Before long we were headed to Salon Persona on Newbury Street. If I were to hashtag this place it would be #SalontotheStars. Anyone who is anyone in Boston has their hair done here. To commemorate her first visit to a high end city salon, mum wore a funky black and white striped, knee-length dress with black leather shoulder accents. The dress had a 1950's flare with modern funk. She felt like a million bucks in this dress.

She looked like another million bucks when her Newbury Street stylist transformed her hair. My eyes well up whenever I picture her twirling around the salon, feeling years lighter once her fresh cut and color was blown out.

After the salon experience we had lunch seated on a window seat in Boston. As she reveled in people watching she said, "Why have I waited so long to feel this way? I know I cannot afford this type of pampering every month. I know most people cannot afford this. But we should be saving up so that *once* a year, people know what it is like to feel this way. Maybe on a birthday. Maybe on an anniversary. We all need to feel this way. We all deserve to be queen for a day."

The sincerity of mum's words made tiny tear pools fill my eyes. I was in a position to drain my savings and max my credit cards to pay for these adventures. I knew I would be able to work extra hours to rebuild the savings and pay off the credit cards once our adventures ended. I realize my situation is atypical. This great gift of financial "freedom" to spoil Wanda is not lost on me.

Wanda continued to gush about the salon experience. "I mean, the fifteen minute head massage at the shampoo station was enough to leave people wanting more. As I approach death I am learning so much about life. About how I wished I had lived all of these years. I feel so grateful for all of this bucket-listing but I feel sad for all of the people who will never make time to live before they die. I have lived more in the past few weeks than I have in my entire life. Oh my God, we have to remember to take a selfie."

She was right. We should all have a mason jar tucked away with spare change. The savings should be for something fun. Fun doesn't have to break the bank. We had plenty of adventures that cost little more than the price of gas in the car, a drive through Dunkin Donuts, and an affordable snack.

One of our favorite low cost adventures is hunting for ghost signs. A ghost sign is an old hand-painted advertising signage that has been preserved on a building for an extended period of time. The signs are often kept for nostalgia. Some ghost signs are left up years after the business has closed and a new business has opened in the same building. This was mum's favorite type of ghost sign. We'd search the factory and downtown districts of cities in Massachusetts hoping to find premiere ghost signs.

Mum submitted all of the photos she took on her iPhone to the Ghost Signs UK Facebook page. Impressed with her finds, the ghost sign lovers of the United Kingdom posted her pics. The posts usually started with "Another beauty from our friend in the USA, Wanda Howard. Thanks!" Whenever her pictures appeared on their page via her newsfeed she would scream. "They posted my ghost sign!"

Team Wanda devoured free museum exhibits, art galleries, trinket shops, joke shops, nature trips, ocean treasure hunting, and haunted hunts. My sister Elizabeth's best friend Jen was an MVP on our team. The girls would pick up mum and drive her through the properties of prison and mental institutions rumored to be haunted. They would do this for hours.

Wanda was a dedicated enthusiast for all things in the spirit world. One day we visited an abandoned, allegedly haunted air force base on Cape Cod. In less than thirty minutes another item was crossed off of the list. Mum's bucket list wasn't filled with big ticket items. Of course she always wanted to see Italy and we tried to get her there, but it wasn't in the cards.

Italy is my one and only bucket listing regret. I should have tried harder to help her eat a plate of pasta while people watching a few paisanos (Italian slang for friend) in Florence. She also wanted to see the art in Florence. I suspect she has the greatest view of the most brilliant art now in heaven. This is what I consider whenever I allow regret about Italy to sneak into my head. I feel confident I will feel my mother's spirit in Florence if I ever make it there. I know she will be waiting for me.

I admired the diversity of mum's bucket list. Many of her final wishes or list items revolved around spending more time with the people she loved in the places she loved.

Some of mum's best memories during the final phase of her life took place on her deck. She had a circle of friends she called the Deck Girls. She even had t-shirts made up with a coffee cup and their title. Mum loved sealing a date with the Deck Girls in pen on her wall calendar in the hallway off of her kitchen. (Her best friend Linda loved poking fun at her for having a wall calendar in an age when most schedules are kept neatly on a phone or iPad.)

It wasn't until mum's terminal diagnosis that she actively engaged in frequent dates with girlfriends. Prior to the cancer metastasizing, mum spent almost all of her time with her daughters and grandchildren.

I loved hearing her talk about the Deck Girls coming over. She'd list every item of food each girl had committed to bringing. "Dawn (a newer friend) is bringing a chicken dish I am dying to try. Sue (a friend since junior high who she had fallen out of touch with) is bringing a dessert that sounds to die for. I will save you some."

We were so grateful mum had friends to confide in. This was yet another life lesson. It is never too late to reestablish life-long friendships or to forge new relationships. Wanda's next bucket list item is one of my favorite examples of this lesson.

<u>Wanda Stairs Howard July 31, 2013 near Boston, MA</u>

Loving life right now walking around Boston with a
nice cool breeze. Close to Mass Gen. Not wandering too
far except to eat across the street and then get my toes
done at Cambridge Nails. Love people watching.

8

Make Art with Beach Treasures

*W*ANDA LOVED MAPS AND HISTORY. MOST of all, she loved any region that was nestled on the ocean. The island of Cuttyhunk was one of her greatest geographic curiosities. Through the years she read a few books about Cuttyhunk, which is the outermost of the Elizabeth Islands in Massachusetts. Some believe it was a lucky coincidence that mum's best friend Linda had a close connection to Cuttyhunk. I believe it was God's way of helping mum experience one of her most desired bucket list wishes.

On a perfect, near end of summer day, Linda hopped in her Mini Cooper and picked up mum. They drove to the ferry and headed toward the island of Cuttyhunk. They were accompanied by a group of women my mother fondly named, "The Cuttyhunk Girls." These girls were directly tied to Cuttyhunk. They either grew up, summered on, or still lived on the island. What better way to experience Cuttyhunk after the summer rush than with life-long islanders?

Although the ferry ride was less than an hour away from Wanda's house, she was so consumed with anticipation, she felt like she was visiting a different part of the world. Greeted by a private golf cart chariot, the girls collected video footage on their iPhones as they were tossed about on the bumpy hills of the island. Listeners can hear my mother laughing in the background of the video clips. Her voice is filled with pure joy.

Wanda spent the entire day touring every inch of the tiny two-and-a-half-mile-long island. She collected treasures on the shore: a piece of an old barge, shells, sand, a puddingstone, pieces of a wire trap. Later she would glue all of these pieces to a beach landscape canvas she painted. She painted Cuttyhunk on the finished product and proudly displayed it on the wall in her living room.

This was extremely out of character for my mother. Her home usually resembled a page out of a magazine. Never would she dream of gluing rocks and sand to a piece of canvas and hanging it. Since her diagnosis mum was doing a lot of things that were totally out of her character.

My all-time favorite pics of mum were taken that day on Cuttyhunk. In one photo she is laying belly down on the damp sand. In the sand beside her are the words Cuttyhunk 2013 are written in the sand. She is wearing a blue hooded sweatshirt over her t-shirt and black leggings. Carefree, barefoot, and smiling ear to ear, one would never know she was dying.

In another photo my mother is leaning up against the old wooden door of Cuttyhunk Cafe. The building is painted gray and mum is wearing an oversized, hot pink, scoop neck, long sleeved t-shirt. The contrast of color is striking. Even more striking is the expression on her face. Her hair is down, her sunglasses are on and her face is looking up toward the sky. This picture boasts one of her widest smiles. The kind of smile she reserved for her happiest moments. This kind of smile revealed her fabulous dimple.

For all of the remaining days of her life, mum referred to September 17, 2013 (her day on Cuttyhunk) as one of the best days of her life. For her entire adult life she was less than an hour away from an island she had always wanted to see. Metastatic cancer is what finally got her there.

Wanda fantasized about returning to the island the following year with us. She spoke about the places she would show us, but she was never able to return. In honor of Wanda, I implore you to stop putting off visits to places that have always piqued your interest. Consider calling someone you love, going to your calendars, and making a date. I know you can make this happen. Consider collecting a bunch of treasures. Maybe you'll feel inspired to use your treasures to tell your story by using them to create wall art.

Wanda continued to make wall art after visiting every beach her final year. By the end of her life the living room wall had a long column of hand-crafted beach art covered in sea glass, shells, sand, baby crab claws, razor clams, and rocks from her findings. Every piece began with a pile of beach collections and a hand-painted, beach-themed canvas. Each daughter was gifted a piece in her final wishes. Her Lighthouse Beach piece now hangs in my kitchen. She painted the name of this stunning beach on a large shell she glued to the canvas.

Seated in her cozy chair a few feet away from her awesome wall art she said, "Who collects treasures on the best beaches, paints canvas, glues all of their best discoveries on the canvas and then hammers nails into their walls to hang the finished product? I mean, really, who does this?"

"You do," I said. "Yes, you are right. But everyone should, don't ya think? Why don't we? Why do we only hang stuff that we think should be on our walls? My beach stuff is way cooler. Every one of these pieces tells a story. When I look at them I remember my day at the beach. This makes me feel very happy."

The next part of our conversation is permanently engraved in my memory. With her feet resting on the leather hassock of her favorite chair and her reading glasses pushed just slightly down her nose, she looked up from her iPad and said, "You know Lorna, end-stage cancer is very liberating. I feel a sense of freedom that I have never felt before. I feel like I can be more honest with people. I can put myself first for the first time in my life. I wake up every day and have something wonderful to look forward to. I can enjoy, really enjoy, every moment with my family and friends. I am so blessed to have this time. Many people never have the chance to experience life from this perspective. Of course, I hate to leave all of you. I worry about leaving the grandkids while they are still so young. I wonder if they will remember me. I know you will all be okay. I thank God every day for what I have right now."

No anger. No pity. At this moment she seemed to be full of peace.

Wanda Stairs Howard August 14, 2013 near Buzzards Bay, MA

So peaceful sitting on the deck listening to the birds
sing their early morning song. Grateful.

9

Buy Comfy Shoes and Get Colorful Tattoos

*W*ANDA HAD BECOME OBSESSED WITH STARFISH. She began correcting people who referred to them as starfish by saying, "Their real name is sea star." Mum identified with the sea star's ability to regenerate damaged parts and shed arms as a means of defense. She shared a sense of resilience with sea stars. Like the sea star, parts of her body had been cut off. Her spirit had to regenerate the areas in which cancer once had lived.

By the end of her life most of her body was made up of damaged parts. The cancer was now in many of her bones which increased her level of pain. Her oncologist added Zometa infusions to her monthly Faslodex injections. This treatment can help reduce and delay bone complications caused by cancer that has spread to the bone. Zometa is not an anti-cancer therapy but it is often used with anti-cancer therapies to make the bones stronger.

The bones in mum's feet were suffering. We needed a comfortable yet stylish shoe to facilitate her day trips and incessant bucket-listing. For many years mum had been reading about hand-stitched, Italian leather shoes known as Tieks. According to their website, "Tieks by Gavrieli are the most versatile designer flats in the world." A short video on the website shows Oprah wearing the shoes. Made of the finest Italian leathers and designed to fold and fit in a purse, their reputation for comfort justified their price.

We were on to our next bucket list challenge. Mum loved the 'fashion- meets- comfort' concept of Tieks. She'd flip through magazines or pass by the far more affordable options in the shoe sections of a department stores saying, "Someday I will save up for Tieks."

Her someday arrived in a striking Tieks blue box with a gorgeous decorative flower on top. The flower was attached to a beautiful wide elastic band covered in fabric, which wrapped around the box. Nestled inside of the box, the ballet slipper shoes patiently waited as mum took her time gently unwrapping each lush layer. I photographed every step of the unveiling. "Are you ready?" she asked as she approached the final layer. "Yes, I am ready. Are *you*?" I said, laughing at her painstakingly long process of putting the darn shoes on her feet.

Her eyes filled up the moment she held the black leather flats. "Oh my God," she said as she discovered the signature Tieks blue stripe going up the back of each shoe. Her Boston accent flew out as she said, "Feel these shoes. They are butter. They feel like butter. This Italian leather is like butter." She was right. The Italian leather was as soft as butter. Wanda held the shoes up to the side of her face and sighed. From there she hugged the shoes.

Since her diagnosis, mum was enforcing longer hugs. She said studies had been done on hugging. Research confirmed that twenty-second hugs release the bonding hormone and neurotransmitter oxytocin, which is nature's form of an antidepressant. As mum hugged the Tieks I began to wonder if she was releasing a bonding hormone on the shoes.

I wondered if this moment with the shoes of her dreams would have felt as profound had it not occurred during the end of her life. When one assumes they have the rest of their life ahead of them do they stop to hug shoes? As an observer of the happiness before me, I vote YES to living in the moment and YES to shoe hugging.

Mum giggled like a little girl as she slipped each shoe over her feet. "I can't believe this is happening! I can't believe they are here." Suddenly it was time for the moment of truth. As she stood from the chair we glanced at one another with anticipation. Were the most versatile designer flats in the world (flats so comfortable the likes of Oprah Winfrey owns pairs in every color) actually comfortable?

In anticipation of the first step I donned my head with the flower from the box, placed across my forehead like a headband from the 1920's, and I stood beside my mother waiting for her first step. The camera setting on my phone was activated. "Here I go," mum said, followed by, "They are perfect! I am walking on air. I am literally walking on air!" I followed her around the kitchen taking photos. "Let's see how they feel on the deck," she said. I kept snapping photos of the shoes, her ankles, and her feet on the deck. "Oh my God, I am so happy. This is epic. These shoes are epic. Epic."

This was the first of many times I heard mum use the word epic that final year of her life. Note to self: Life is too short...buy the shoes. Mum sent copies of the pictures of her feet in the Tieks to them and even inboxed them on Facebook. The following day she sent this email:

-----Original Message-----
From: Wanda Howard [mailto:wandamarie7@comcast.net]
Sent: Sunday, September 15, 2013 8:52 AM
To: Lorna
Subject: Tieks

All my comments and pics made it to the Tieks homepage!!!

To make life even more epic mum decided to do something she said she would never "in a million years" do. She made an appointment to get a starfish/sea star tattoo. Growing up in the 1970's in my mother's home we were told that tattoos were for "whores, sailors, or bikers." Good girls didn't get inked. End of story.

Imagine my shock and awe when mum, her best friend Linda, my sisters, my niece and family friend Jen rolled into a tattoo parlor to become branded by sister sea stars. A sucker for mum's house rules, I did not get a tatt.

Wanda lovingly called her first tattoo her "ugly starfish." A blend of orange, gold and black, the ugly starfish sat off center on her right forearm. Her artist's eye was unhappy with the lack of detail in the starfish tattoo, she had expected more definition and contrast. The artwork clearly wasn't good enough or she would have named the tatt her sea star. "It is what it is," she'd say whenever she looked at the ugly starfish. I think she saw the flawed tattoo as a metaphor for life's imperfections.

That said, the perfectionist in mum seemed to want a perfect tattoo on her skin. So she went back to a well-known, high end parlor managed by my cousin Jon. The tattoo artist inked a rosary bead around mum's ankle with three favorite things: a lighthouse, a cross, and a starfish. The light of hope, faith and resilience. At last mum had a perfect sea star on her body.

Conversations about her next tattoo began almost immediately. She wanted to honor her grandchildren in the next tattoo, so she returned to the parlor and on the opposite side of the ugly starfish, on the inside of her forearm, she inscribed all four of the children's names, Paige, Tyler, Taylor, and Trey. Underneath she had them write "Love You More." This is a saying she used to say to all of the children before bedtime. They'd say "I love you" and she'd reply "I love you more" and after she'd say "to the moon and back." Pillows with each of the expressions rested on the couch in her living room. Almost every text I have saved from my mother ended with "love you more."

She got the stink eye a few times from people who most likely grew up in households that thought tattoos were for whores, sailors and bikers. If ever this happened, mum would proudly say, "These are my end-of-life tattoos. I am dying of breast cancer. I wanted the names of my grandchildren on my body when I die. They are my world. I spent too much time judging, too much time worrying about what people would think if I had a tattoo. Now that I am at the end of my life all that really matters is what I need, what I want. I want to get a fourth tattoo commemorating my three daughters. After that, I may get a koi fish. By then I will have a sleeve."

Mum's tattoo speech usually either converted or further horrified the people brazen enough to stare at her skin. Despite her beauty and kind heart, Wanda had quite a way with words. Her Sicilian temper could go from zero to ten in seconds. I pitied the people who looked down their nose at something as silly as her tattoo. It was seldom that mum practiced verbal restraint.

Mum's final tattoo was the most beautiful. The artist designed a beautiful woman with long flowing hair that had seashells running through it. The base of her neck had three large pink hibiscus flowers, three flowers for her three girls. The shades of purple, red, blue and pink in this tattoo were especially breathtaking.

These end-of-life tattoos made mum very happy. Her skin became her gallery. As a lover of art, this was one of the greatest things she had ever done for herself. Please pursue things that will bring you great joy. Whether it is a pair of shoes that you have always wanted, a full sleeve of tattoos, or a discretely hidden tiny tattoo, please make a promise to yourself to do something epic.

<u>Wanda Stairs Howard August 20, 2013 near Buzzards Bay, MA</u>

You know the expression, It happens once in a blue moon? Well first thing happened was me getting a tattoo and now I just beat Level 65 in Candy Crush!! Thank you blue moon.

10

Preserve Your Voice on Video

$\mathcal{W}$ITH MUM'S AWESOME NEW NEWBURY STREET haircut and the recent chat we had about the grandchildren remembering her, it seemed like a great time for a cool project. We called my friend and asked her to bring her video camera to mum's house. Our goal was to record a legacy video of mum. This was our way of guaranteeing the grandchildren would not forget her. Through this video, her future great-grandchildren would have the chance to hear her beautiful voice, see her contagious smile, and experience the overall essence and spirit of mum.

The day before the video shoot my sisters and I, along with the grandkids, wrote lists of questions we wanted her to answer on film. We compiled pages of questions. The questions ranged from "Who was your first kiss?" to "How do you make your famous Italian chicken cutlets?" or "What makes you the most happy?"

Coming from an Italian family, it is no surprise that many of the questions were about how she prepared food. There were few to no recipes in our kitchen growing up. Mum made everything by taste and learned from watching others cook. On the legacy video mum walked us through her stuffed artichokes, perfectly pounded paper-thin chicken cutlets, tomato sauce, and rice pilaf.

For hours she answered questions, offered advice, shared life lessons, and spoke directly to us about subjects that were paramount in her life. Happiness was one of the most important topics. She spoke a lot about the necessity of happiness. This topic branched into the importance of mental health. Mum's mother battled depression and alcoholism when mum was a little girl. Mum wanted us to be sure to seek help the moment feelings of despair crept in. "Life's too short to feel angry or sad," she said with a big smile on her face. "There are people who can help, but you have to be honest with yourself before anyone can help you."

As the mother of three girls and the grandmother of two girls, she spoke about hot flashes, hormones and menopause. Naturally, she included the importance of annual mammograms. She spoke about the various stages of love, commenting on the difference between temporary and permanent love, and she vocalized a green light for any of us who needed to move on to new relationships if there wasn't enough healthy love in the home. She spoke of the importance of independence and financial stability.

On the topic of love, she thanked her husband Doug for allowing her to find her way after her first cancer diagnosis in 2009. During the year that followed mum's recovery she found herself searching for greater meaning in her life. She realized she had never been on her own. At seventeen years old, she had me and was married. She never had her own apartment or lived alone in a home without children or a man. In order to evolve, she needed to give solitude a try.

We helped mum move into a nice studio apartment about twenty minutes away from the home she shared with her husband. They weren't divorcing or even breaking up, they were just agreeing to give mum some room to breathe. For the first time in her life she only watched what she wanted to watch on TV. She rented the movies only she wanted to rent. She ate the meals only she wanted to eat. She shut off the bedroom light when only she was finished reading or ready to fall asleep. She cleaned up after only herself. She did the laundry for no one but herself. She shopped for food for only herself. She decided when there was sound and when there was silence.

She was by no means a hermit in her studio apartment. She saw one or all of us almost every day. She saw her husband quite a bit, too. By living alone, she faced and overcame many fears. I loved watching her evolve during the year she lived on her own. She developed an independent pride that I hadn't noticed before. There was an overall ease about her. She smiled constantly and exuded more confidence.

When the year-long lease was up she returned home. Just before the lease ended, mum called one night saying she was having a hard time walking and a MRI in Boston showed fluid in her hip. They suggested her autoimmune issues were to blame. With anti-inflammatory meds the hip effusion went away just as fast as it came. I often wonder if she went back home because the hip incident caused her to panic about growing older, and perhaps sicker, alone. I prefer to think she left the studio because she had learned the answers to all of her questions and was able to check "silent soul–searching" off of her to-do list.

Either way, mum thanked Doug on the legacy video and made sure he understood what his sacrifice meant to her. She concluded her message to him by saying, "There aren't many men who would allow their wives to move out, who would help them move, no questions asked, continue to support them the year they are gone, and welcome them back when they want to return home. This was a very important time for me. I needed to be alone. Thank you for understanding me and for loving me."

The "power of one" was another life lesson mum instilled in us. She said it was important to find a safe space in your own company. She encouraged all of her daughters to embrace alone time. From reading a book, to floating away in the bathtub, mum appreciated the restorative benefits of being alone.

The legacy video is one of the smartest decisions we made during the final year of Wanda's life. One of the questions we asked was about mum's love of music and singing. Through the years she had credited her Aunt Rose for singing lullabies to her as a child. Mum always ended our days with a lullaby. "Shake Me I Rattle," was our most requested tune and the song Aunt Rose used to sing to mum. There is a moment on the video where mum sings a piece of the song. At the end of the video Colleen streamed a bunch of photos of mum with all of us and played the full-length version of "Shake Me I Rattle."

Mum also tells us that we are only allowed to be sad for one day once she has died. She warns us of how sad she will feel if she checks in on us only to find that we are crying and missing her. She asks that we try our hardest to laugh, joke, and celebrate life once she has gone. Hour after hour on camera she hit home run life lessons out of the park.

Although we made the video for the little children, mum's husband Doug watches the video a lot. I ask that you not wait until someone you love is sick before making a legacy video. Please call anyone with a video camera or a decent smart phone and begin recording moments of the people you love. I know too many people who have lost loved ones and don't have so much as a voicemail to remember the sound of their voice. When I see my mother looking gorgeous on her legacy video, laughing and sharing stories about her life, I am charged with emotion. I wouldn't give this video up for all of the money in the world. Of course my absolute favorite part of the video is what mum said *after* she watched herself on the video.

"Hi, it's me. I just watched the video. Some parts are long, but most parts are good. I look pissa. (Boston slang for excellent.) My hair looks epic. Seriously, I should have been a news broadcaster or something. I seriously could have hosted my own talk show. People would have watched. I'm pretty awesome." *Yes you are, mum. You are pretty awesome.*

Wanda Stairs Howard August 12, 2013 near Middleboro, MA

I put all my eggs in one basket and gave the basket to God.

11

Make Time to Be Silly

S A TEAM WE MADE SURE mum always had something in both the near and distant future to look forward to. My niece Paige had always wanted to see Salem, Massachusetts. To celebrate her twenty-first birthday, we planned an August trip for Paige, mum, and I to visit the place where modern-day witches walk freely. We booked a hotel that is rumored to be haunted.

Mum had treatments at the hospital in Boston scheduled the week prior to our Salem trip. Her cocktails, Faslodex and Zometa, were served at the crack of dawn. The day before her treatment we checked into the hotel near the hospital. While in the city mum wanted to visit her friend Jeanne. As adorable Italian children they grew up on opposites sides of the same street in Watertown, Massachusetts. In mum's eyes, Jeanne was family. Jeanne's sister Sharyn is godmother to me and my sister Elizabeth.

Jeanne and mum had more than a life-long friendship in common. In 2009, both girls had to show cancer who was boss; mum with breast and Jeanne with lung. They laughed at each other as their hair "chemo curl" grew in after treatments. Jeanne marveled at the rebellious nature of my mother when she decided to dye her pure white, inch-long hair brown weeks before the doctors recommended it. "You hot ticket" she'd say looking at my mother's short, brown and perfectly gelled post-chemo hair. "You are a riot."

Cut ahead five years later to July 2013. My mother is lying in a bed with tubes all over her in Boston a few floors above the room Jeanne is sitting in having chemo. The cancer had metastasized in both girls. Jeanne and her daughter visited mum after chemo.

"Well, hello," mum said as she greeted her friend. This was followed by both women building each other up with streaming praise. "You look *wonderful*," Jeanne said, as she held my mother's hand. "Still *gorgeous*," my mother replied and then added, "I love your hair." "Would 'ya look at us. Of all the places to meet up," Jeanne said.

I treasure a photo of the two of them. Jeanne is sitting next to mum's hospital bed and they are laughing hysterically. They knew they were dying, but as women of faith, neither of their faces showed any sadness. Their trust in God seemed to fortify them from fear. With so little time left, they were two old friends having a visit, living in the moment. "Hey, we have to keep laughing, right?" Jeanne said to Wanda. "It certainly is better than crying." This visit took place in July.

In August (the night before Wanda's treatment) we went to visit Jeanne at her home. Looking as stunning as ever, she rested peacefully. Mum sat alone with Jeanne for a few moments before we kissed her and said goodbye. When we got in the car my mother said, "I asked her to be waiting for me when I get to heaven. I told her it won't be long until we are together again."

The next morning mum and I dressed in our hotel and prepared for our day at the hospital. Mum went ahead of me to get her morning coffee in the hotel lobby. A few minutes later I found my mother sitting in a corner of the lobby crying. "She's gone. Jeanne died this morning. I am so glad she waited for me to say goodbye."

For the next hour Wanda was inconsolable. Through tears she conveyed her need for us to prepare for the inevitable. "You see why we have to live every day to the fullest? Jeanne was visiting *me* in the hospital less than a month ago. She seemed strong. I didn't think she was so close to the end. We were just laughing together. Things happen so quickly at the end. You have to prepare. Everyone has to prepare to expect this with me. I can be here today, laughing and bucket-listing and I can be gone tomorrow."

There was a shift in Wanda's energy. Jeanne and mum had won in 2009. Now, her dear friend was gone. The circumstances were different. It was less easy to hold on to hope for longevity. Mum's medical team never put a timeline on her life expectancy. They said things like, "With Faslodex I have seen people in your condition live from 18 months up to five years. Anything is possible." The week after Jeanne's death mum sent us emails with hard facts about how much time she had left.

Girls,

I don't want this email to upset any of you, but I think we need to be practical. Elizabeth Edwards had my exact cancer. She is no longer with us. I am eventually going to die. You need to prepare for this. In most cases people with my type of advanced cancer don't live past 18 months. Rather than be sad, let's make the most out of this time. Let's be grateful for this extra time. Time that so many people never have. All day. Every day.

I love you all to the moon and back,
Mom Xo

The following week we went to Salem. We bucket-listed and made memories. One day all three of us suited up in head to toe elaborate witch costumes and took photos flying on a broom through the sky. We did this in one of those keepsake studios. Mum kept staring at our photos saying, "Look at how awesome we look. These photos are epic. We look epic. I am so glad we did this for Paige's birthday. Making memories is EPIC. You will have these photos forever. You have to post them in October on your Facebook pages. Epic."

A few weeks later mum planned her entire funeral. She went to the funeral home and took care of everything. Music selections, readings, poems, and funny stories were perfectly placed in a box with instructions. She plainly called the box her funeral box. The week of the planning, I drove her to Winston's flowers to select her casket spray and funeral flowers.

Mum was very particular about what she wanted for flowers. "I love flowers," she said. "They have to be perfect. I want people to remember how beautiful the flowers were. This is important to me." Mum was born in a time when donations to charities "In lieu of flowers" wasn't a thing. She was extremely charitable but loved her flowers. In some ways her old school mind measured the love of loved ones who had passed by how many flowers were displayed in the funeral home. To her, flowers were literally a visual sign of love.

By the second week of September mum's death arrangements had been planned. From there she carried on with living. Mum spoke of Jeanne almost every day until they were reunited in heaven. We know Jeanne was there waiting for her.

Mum was right about the photos of us dressed up as witches. We do look awesome in every shot. We love looking at them now, especially since she has returned to heaven. Be sure to make time to be silly. Put a witch hat on and fly through an imaginary sky. Giggle in your hospital bed during a visit with an old friend. Make memories that will make you smile for years to come.

<u>Wanda Stairs Howard</u> <u>August 26, 2013</u>

Remember the memories that you've made in life, think of them often, that way you get to enjoy the experiences more than just once!

12

It's Never Too Late to Try Something New

WANDA WAS FULL SPEED AHEAD WITH the adventures and day trips. Shortly after her Cuttyhunk trip I hosted a luncheon for all of the Cuttyhunk Girls. This was mum's way of thanking them for an epic day on the island. Platters of fried chicken were bookended by bowls of potato salad and coleslaw. I loved hearing mum laugh with her new friends. Wanda had cooked meals for me and my friends during my entire childhood. It felt awesome to give back a tiny piece of this ritual in return.

A few days after the luncheon, my friend Susan offered Wanda another ocean adventure. Susan is connected to a wonderful organization called Sailing Heals. Sailing Heals is a non-profit organization that partners with sailors to offer VIP patient guests and their caregivers a memorable day of healing on the water. Two tickets had just become available for the final sail of the season. Susan knew Wanda would benefit from a day on the ocean.

On October 6, 2013, during Columbus Day weekend, we stepped aboard the classic sailing yacht, Madeleine. The 72-foot schooner sailing yacht was specifically designed and built to carry passengers easily and safely sailing through the local waters of Newport, Rhode Island. The yacht is the perfect combination of 19th century sailboat style with 21st century sailing yacht comfort and convenience.

Mum was overwhelmed with excitement. I had never seen her so happy. After a lifelong affair with the sea, Wanda had found her love. She ran her hands across every part of the yacht. "Isn't it the most beautiful thing you have ever seen? I cannot believe this. I just can't get over it." Although I appreciated Madeleine's beauty, I was concerned about mum slipping into the water once the vessel tilted in the wind.

"You need to relax," mum repeated as we sailed away from the harbor, "there is nothing to worry about." At this point mum was on a very high dose of steroids. She was jumpier than usual. I was concerned that her adrenaline and excitement would mix with the steroids and lead to a "King of The World" moment at the bow of the boat.

As always, mum was right, I needed to relax. Once I settled into the idea of freeing myself from worry, I joined my mother and together we fell in love with sailing. I have over fifty photos of my mother drinking in every moment of her time with Madeleine. Not since her diagnosis had I seen her shoulders so relaxed. All of her neck and upper back tension seemed to drift away with every wave that crashed beneath the vessel.

"I feel wonderful," she said smiling at me. "Have you ever felt this free? I wish we could do this every weekend. I want to get the kids out here. I want them to feel this. I want them to learn how to sail. Why on earth did we wait so long to try this?"

As she spoke we sailed past some of the most affluent homes in Newport, Rhode Island. Our favorite was Hammersmith Farm. The Victorian mansion was the childhood home of Jacqueline Bouvier Kennedy Onassis. The property hosted the wedding reception of Jackie and John F. Kennedy. The view of this property from the water was stunning.

"I feel so at peace," my mother said looking out at the water. As one of my mother's care providers, I had been on high alert for months. Be that as it may, I couldn't help becoming lost in the near perfect moment.

With mum's gorgeous hair blowing in the breeze I was able to seal her tranquil beauty in my mind. In this moment, my mother didn't have cancer. She wasn't sick. She wasn't in pain. She wasn't dying. She was living in perfect harmony with God through nature.

For a long while I leaned my back up against her back as we sailed along. At first I did this to make sure she was securely seated. After a while, I remained in this position because I loved feeling her relaxed body leaning up against mine. I could literally feel her deep and happy breaths expanding through her back. Her joyful energy captured the hearts of everyone aboard.

A man named Dan was especially moved by mum's poise and solace in the face of a terminal illness. Dan is a writer for Yachting Magazine who was on assignment to cover the therapeutic benefits of Sailing Heals. He sat with my mother for much of the sail talking about life and cancer. Two months later a darling photo of mum and I appeared in the 2013 December Holiday issue of Yachting Magazine.

Near the picture, the following words were written by Dan about my mother. "One guest, Wanda Howard, sits on the companionway hatch with a smile stretching from ear to ear. "Four years ago I didn't live life to the fullest," she says softly while glancing around the boat. "Now that I have stage-four cancer, I appreciate things like this so much more." The article goes on to mention that "Sailing Heals has taken nearly 600 cancer patients and caregivers sailing in the hope of providing an escape, however brief, from their pain."

Shortly after our afternoon at sea had ended, mum began collecting literature for summer sailing lessons for the grandchildren. With winter approaching, she placed the pamphlets in a pile vowing to make sure the kids discovered what it feels like to fly on water. Decorative sailboats joined the ranks of her beloved sea stars and sand dollars in her kitchen and living room. One night she said, "Sailing is one of my most favorite things. We should never have waited so long to try it. We need to sail a lot more next summer. I am serious about this."

If you have any way to make it happen, I wholeheartedly encourage all of you to add sailing to your bucket list. Please be sure to think of Wanda when the wind fills the sails.

Wanda Stairs Howard September 21, 2013 · Buzzards Bay, MA ·

To my friends who are having a luncheon on Friday...listen up...
No one is to bring anything, understood? No one
brings food to an Italian house because it's an insult.
Capiche? Thank you for your support. LOL

13

If You Want to Find the Tastiest Food Ask the Locals

ALTHOUGH MUM TOOK TO SAILING LIKE a mermaid takes to water, deep down inside she always prided herself in being more of a fishing boat kind of girl. Her favorite reality TV show was Deadliest Catch, a docudrama that portrays the real life events aboard fishing vessels in the Bering Sea during the crab fishing seasons.

One of mum's favorite books was The Perfect Storm by Sebastian Junger. The book is about the crew of the swordfishing boat named the *Andrea Gail* that got caught in the Perfect Storm of 1991. Many of the crew members were from Gloucester, Massachusetts.

Shortly after seeing the movie version of The Perfect Storm mum visited a local watering hole for the fishermen called The Crow's Nest, located in the heart of the working Gloucester waterfront. Mum was right at home conversing with the regulars about life at sea. She loved the weathered skin of each person seated at the bar. She knew each leathery, sun-kissed face had a story to tell.

Mum loved sharing her stories of sitting on a bar stool at The Crow's Nest. When she recounted the story it was as if she had grown up on a big 'ol fishing boat. She was one of the guys. She was so enamored by the fishing industry she swore she was a captain of a boat or lived in a coastal fishing community in another life.

Her instructions were clear. When she died we were to scatter a portion of her ashes in the sea off her beloved Gloucester and in the neighboring town of Rockport, Massachusetts. Her final resting place would be the sea.

Seaside scattering of cremation remains was nothing new to us. We buried a portion of mum's father's ashes in the National Cemetery in Massachusetts and the rest of his ashes were scattered on Nantasket Beach in Hull, Massachusetts. We scattered a portion of his sister's ashes (Aunt June) in Scituate, Massachusetts in the ocean near a lighthouse.

I was on vacation the week of Columbus Day during mum's final year on earth. A bucket list item was to stay in a home directly on the water with her family. That September I began making calls to a few friends I knew in Gloucester. "We'd kill two birds with one stone," mum said. "We can find the exact spot I'd like to be scattered." Mum loved Good Harbor Beach in Gloucester. During low tide beach, lovers are able to walk across the ocean floor to Salt Island. This was one of mum's favorite places to search for beach treasures.

In 2009 when mum was sick we gathered the family on Old Silver Beach in Falmouth, Massachusetts for a family photo. The very next day mum's hair began falling out from chemo. I wanted another family photo of us, five years later, on mum's new favorite beach.

After making a few calls my friend referred us to a family who hadn't yet closed up their home for the season. We were all set to arrive at the house over the course of the weekend, only mum and I were able to block off the entire week.

On the advice of a friend we agreed to rent the home sight unseen. Although very charming, the house was on a cove, not the open ocean. We overcame this disappointment by having one absolutely perfect day at Good Harbor Beach. For hours we strolled the beach. At low tide in ankle deep water we crossed the chilly sand to Salt Island. Mum was happiest near salt and sand.

I was able to snap my all-time favorite photo of mum and my sister Elizabeth during this excursion. In the photo they are standing between the divide of Salt Island and Good Harbor Beach and the tide is making its way back in. Mum and Elizabeth are smiling and sideways hugging in the sand. This was another one of our priceless moments when cancer played second fiddle to joy.

Mum found a fantastic large piece of driftwood (drift tree is more accurate) along the shore, and we staged a photo of Team Wanda sitting on and around the drift tree. In the photo, everyone is happy. Everyone is grateful for our near perfect day.

After our time on the beach mum had the caravan of cars pull over in front of The Crow's Nest. She escorted the newbies on our trip into her hang out. Watching the industrial fishing boats drift into the harbor she said, "I wish I had lived here for a little while during my life. I don't mean for years, maybe just a season or a month or two. I think people should try living in a foreign place at least once in their life. You learn a lot when you leave your comfort zone."

Mum loved asking the local people of any community for recommendations for the best food. Inevitably their suggestions landed us at a little hole in the wall with five-star food. Mum's favorite place to eat in Gloucester was The Causeway. That night all fifteen of us had an epic New England feast on fresh lobster, clams, scallops, and haddock. Mum was a fan of their flawless lobster pie. Made with lumps of lobster meat, butter and bit of breadcrumbs, this dish can make the knees of a sea captain weak.

Mum collected a great deal of treasures during our days at the ocean. A new piece of wall art was days away from construction. The sea glass, shells and beach photos portray a perfect week on the water. To be honest, we cut our trip short. The closer mum came to her death, the more aware she became of the spirit world. Mum believed the souls of the afterlife had a stronger connection to people who were close to dying.

We left the house rental because we believed the home was haunted. It was clear the spirits didn't want to share the space with us. I'm certain the non-believers will think I am crazy. I'm certain the believers will have similar stories to share. After trying to brush off one too many unwanted signs, we packed up our things and left. Our mother always followed her instinct. The Mama Bear in her needed to protect her family. We loved this about her. Mum always had our backs.

As our car turned away from the house mum said, "I'm not sure if I want to be scattered here after all. I mean, I have loved it here for years, but I am just not sure. What do you think?" she asked. "I think you will know where you want to be buried when the time is right," I said, hoping there was some truth in my words. "Trust your heart."

<u>Wanda Stairs Howard October 27, 2013 near Buzzards Bay, MA</u>

Love the ocean. Some of my finds today.
The sand there has black glitter in it and shines so pretty.

14

Life's Too Short to Settle

*S*OME OF MUM'S FRIENDS ORGANIZED A karaoke party in her honor. The party was held at a local spot where years prior mum worked on weekends as a DJ. Team Wanda represented in strong numbers. The morning of the party mum woke up with one of her worst flare–ups, her entire leg was doubled in size. Her knee hardly bent and her ankle looked like a balloon.

She cried a lot that morning. "I really want to go but I am in terrible pain. I can't walk. I don't want to disappoint anyone. Who knows when I will see everyone again all at once while I am alive."

We called her doctor. He recommended that we double-up the steroid to reduce the inflammation. She also doubled up the pain medication. After spending several hours elevating her leg she decided to attend the party. The only catch...she needed a walker to hold herself up. "It isn't for forever, it is for today. I either use the walker or stay home."

Wearing a white lace shirt, black pants, and flip flops (because her foot was too swollen for a shoe) she entered the restaurant hunched over her walker. With perfect hair, makeup, and jewelry she looked gorgeous.

Despite all of the smoke and mirrors, this was the first time our friends saw her as being sick.

Mum made jokes about the walker and her puffy leg. "Of all the days to have my biggest flare-up my body picks the day my friends have a party for me. Murphy's law." One by one, friends pulled us aside asking questions we should have been asked months prior. "So...how is she *really* doing? Have the doctors given you a timeframe?"

I remember feeling very sad that night. Mum looked fabulous in all of her Facebook photos, but she was always very clear about her terminal illness. Somehow the image of her being hunched over on a walker and the image of people bending over to hug her while she remained seated in a chair hit home. *Wow, she is really sick. She is actually dying.*

The room full of people finally began to process what mum was trying to prepare us for all along. This shift in energy, this epiphany of the inevitable broke my heart. "Wanda the Unstoppable" was beginning to slow down. Was it really the beginning of the end?

The Belle of the Ball, mum didn't let the pain prevent her from enjoying a night with the people she loved. From her table, seated in a chair, she held a cordless mic and sang all of her hits. "Turn Back Time" by Cher is the song that brought people to their feet that night. The concept of turning back time was both poignant and powerful.

One by one her friends took the mic and serenaded her with songs from the decades of her life. I have three favorite photos from this night. In one photo mum is seated in a chair on stage and her husband Doug and her friends Roger and Billy are standing around her singing "In the Still of the Night." She is smiling from ear to ear.

In another photo my mother is seen standing right next to a chair on stage. She is supporting her weight by holding the mic stand. She is standing tall and singing her heart out as if to say "Screw you, cancer. Screw you, walker. Screw you pain. I am standing up and singing." My final favorite photo of the night is a group shot of all of us standing around mum and Doug, who remained seated in two chairs in the center. Love literally shines off of the photo. For real. In many ways this night was mum's living funeral. It was the last time her friends heard her sing.

The elevated levels of steroids prescribed to reduce the latest flare-up in her leg did a number on my mother. She was racing non-stop. This madness went on for weeks. Brief cat naps were her only form of sleep. She never slept soundly. She never rested. She never restored her energy.

With mum wrapped in a blanket, resting her head on a pillow in the back seat of my Jeep, I drove her into Boston for her next appointment. In addition to the scheduled Faslodex and Zometa, we wanted to discuss a plan. We wanted to reduce the steroids and restore her ability to rest. The side effects of the life-prolonging medications were squelching her quality of life.

Mum's oncologist was stumped by the way her body was reacting to the meds. He claimed that he had never seen flare-ups in his other patients. Perhaps the other patients didn't have autoimmune issues? A sleepless and emotionally exhausted version of Wanda the warrior began to cry during the appointment.

This wasn't the first time her doctor had seen her cry. As a caregiver, I sensed how frustrated mum's doctor had become. As a daughter, I sensed how skeptical my mother had become in his ability to help or understand her. The relationship was no longer working. It knew it was time for a change.

An hour later we sat at mum's favorite Italian restaurant Antonio's across the street from the hospital. As regulars during her treatments, the waiters knew our order. Two ziti and meatball lunches with a salad. Dressing: Olive oil, balsamic vinegar, and oregano. Bread with real butter not olive oil. Parmesan cheese on the table. Two cannolis. One coffee with extra creamers and two ice waters with lemon.

As we waited for our lunch, mum recounted the appointment with her doctor and became extremely emotional. She was dissatisfied with her level of care. She listed reasons why she was unhappy with her oncologist. This list included him hollering at her on the phone the week prior, cutting her off mid-sentence during the appointments, ignoring her plea to obtain sleep by reducing the steroids and his lack of knowledge regarding the root cause of her joint flare ups.

I promised we would chisel away at each issue she had with the doctor and encouraged her to take a mental break from the hospital and focus on our yummy lunch. My advice escalated her anger. Her voice grew louder as she pounded the table with her fists. "This is *my* damn body! *My* damn cancer! If I decided to stop treatment, it is *my* decision. If I decide to be done with the hospital and doctors, it is *my* decision. *My* damn decision! Got it?"

This wasn't the first time her cancer frustration presented in the form of butt kicking. I was a safe place to empty her anger and fear. In my company, she was allowed to shove a flag into the dirt and claim her sovereignty. If banging her fists on the table helped her hold onto her life, I was happy to remain calm and supportive.

The difference this particular day was my reaction to her rage. As I watched my mother, overloaded on steroids and fuming through fear, tears spurted out of my eyes. I tried to gather the right words to defuse her pain but my sobs prevented me from speaking. I knew she was right. It was time to find another doctor. A lot of this research would fall on my shoulders. For a brief moment, the enormity of the next step got the best of me.

"Oh, come on," she said as I cried. "We have a lot longer to ride this thing out. You are going to have to toughen up. We cannot do this with you being so emotional. I have to be able to have a bad moment in front of you girls. You have to let me be real around you. You need to work on having a thicker skin. Things are going to become a lot worse down the road. Be more rugged. You are strong. Don't forget it."

And just like that, lunch was served and everything was back to normal. As normal as things can be when you are sprinkling parmesan cheese over your pasta, seated across the table from your best friend, who just happens to be dying of cancer.

At first we thought switching to a female oncologist at the same hospital was the answer. Assuming a woman would better understand the emotional journey through breast cancer, I reached out to the proper people to line mum up with a new doctor. One would think this would have been easy. Sadly, the process was more stressful than I ever imagined. We encountered one road block after another.

Mum had one final treatment at the hospital. When the treatment was over, we collected all of her images and reports and said goodbye to the team that twice saved her life. We ceremoniously stood outside of the hospital and said farewell. As we stood on the sidewalk mum thanked her surgeon for saving her in 2009. She thanked the team who saved her by draining and sealing her lung in July of 2013. She thanked all of the nurses and techs who cared for her. "It has been quite a ride. A reason, a season or a lifetime. My reason here has ended and it is time for me to move on."

She walked over to her favorite hospital security person named Mack. They hugged and cried as she said goodbye. I have a beautiful photo of them embracing. You can see their bond in their eyes. "I love you, mum," he said in his island accent. "God bless 'ya, mum."

We came full circle with our nostalgia by eating one last time at mum's favorite Italian restaurant. No menu necessary. Two ziti and meatball lunches with a salad. The difference this day, we didn't order two take-out cannolis for our hotel room. After the meal we were headed home.

During lunch mum said, "Always remember you have options. You are never caged in or locked in to anything. Life is about change. You have the right to change. We live in a country that has the best medical options available to us. If the relationship is no longer working...if it is taking away from your happiness...if you are no longer confident that the fit is right...it is okay to move on. It is okay to want and to expect the best. Life's too short to settle."

Next stop, The Dana-Farber Cancer Institute.

Wanda Stairs Howard October 17, 2013 near Buzzards Bay, MA

Sitting on the deck with my morning coffee and realizing it's going to be another beautiful day. This weather has been amazing.

15

You Are Never Too Old For Halloween

WE STAYED IN THE CITY THE night before we met mum's new team at the Dana-Farber Cancer Institute. The Dana-Farber Cancer Institute is a world-renowned cancer treatment and research center in Boston, Massachusetts. It is a teaching affiliate of Harvard Medical School. Before checking into our hotel we picked up a few additional medical files and images at the other hospital.

Mum wanted to have an early supper at a local cafe on Charles Street. As we ate we became surrounded by petite fairies, witches, and goblins. It was Halloween in Boston. To be more specific, it was Halloween on Beacon Hill. Unbeknownst to us, on October 31ˢᵗ the streets of the affluent neighborhoods are blocked off for a huge, high-end Halloween block party.

With her walking stick in hand mum insisted that we walk every cobblestone alley and every hilly sidewalk on Beacon Hill. Residents ran fog machines and hung lights that flashed in orange, purple, and white. Creepy music played as adults dressed in costumes sat in their doorways drinking wine and handing out candy.

"This is so epic!" Mum would say as we traveled through the hill. "We have to take the kids here next year. Who knew this celebration was so epic?" Mum admired all of the adults for submerging themselves in the spirit of the season. She especially loved trick-or-treating in Louisburg Square at The Secretary of State's house. "Let's see what kind of candy John Kerry gives out," she said as we approached his doorstep.

A little voice inside of my head thought *should we really be trick-or-treating? We don't have any children with us.* Those thoughts were quickly overcome by the look of pure joy on Wanda's face. In this perfect moment she was once again an eight-year-old girl trick-or-treating in her childhood city. Knowing this could very well be mum's last Halloween on earth who was I to advise against this harmless escape from terminal cancer?

As mum made her way through the uneven streets of one of the most historic parts of Boston, I knew her body was exhausted. I also knew that she would not agree to return to the hotel until she had seen every inch of the action. Wanda was never one to miss out on the fun. When I asked if she was tired she said, "I can sleep when I am in my coffin. I want to stay longer." Although I hated hearing her use this expression she made a good point.

"I am so happy!" mum exclaimed. "This is one of the best nights ever. Adventure is hiding around every corner. Some days you don't even have to look for it because adventure finds you. How lucky are we to be experiencing this night? How cool are the people opening their homes and offering this to the kids?"

Some thirty years prior mum *was* that person. Every Halloween she would decorate the house, bake and frost cupcakes to look like pumpkin jack-o-lanterns, and dress her children and herself in fabulous costumes. Most of our costumes were handmade. For example, one year we were Indians. Mum's DNA breakdown was Sicilian, Penobscot Indian, and style. She had several wardrobe pieces to compliment her native heritage.

Our Indian costumes were constructed with 1970's brown suede vests and skirts with fringe, suede boots with fur accents, turquoise and silver necklaces wrapped in rows around our necks, earth stone rings on our fingers, and feathers poking through the braids in our hair. We. Looked. Bad. Ass. Mum looked like Pocahontas.

If MTV were around back then, Cher could have made a music video for her song "Half Breed" using our family pics from that Halloween as B-roll footage for the video. You can imagine how awesome we looked the Halloween that fell during mum's gypsy fashion phase. Scarves, bracelets and peasant skirts anyone?

Mum's signature Halloween look was a glamorous character she created named Wanda the Witch. Dressed in beautiful black dresses with long, shiny black wigs, mum was a wickedly pretty witch. She covered every finger in rings and painted her face with makeup that even Elvira Mistress of the Dark would envy.

As much as I loved dressing up on Halloween, my greatest excitement was seeing Wanda the Witch. Mum was one of the only adults who dressed up. In our eyes, this made her more awesome than the other moms.

If you have little ones please remember that children drink in everything that happens around them. When I think of Halloween now some three decades later I don't think of the candy or my costumes. I think of how cool Wanda looked dressed up walking door to door by our side. I think about her willingness to put everything aside to join us and share our joy. She wasn't an observer of our lives, she was an active participant.

Despite mum's illness it seemed odd that Halloween had caught me by surprise that night on Beacon Hill. The weeks leading up to Halloween mum's kitchen and deck table were covered with large white plaster skulls. Mum got everyone together to work on a Sugar Skull arts and crafts project. Mum had an expansive selection of paint, silk flowers, glitter, crystals, and gemstones for epic hours of decorating.

Wanda was brilliant at finding ways to gather everyone around. This forum enabled her to discuss whatever was on her mind. The adults in our crew came to know these gatherings as "family meetings." Whenever she called a meeting to order, we filed in to take note of her message.

When it came to involving the children her family meetings had a more creative flair. Some meetings involved cooking or baking, others involved nature walks or arts and crafts. The topic on mum's mind this time was how to begin a dialogue about her death. She wanted the children to know that she wasn't going to be gone forever. She wanted them to know she would always be able to feel love for them and even see them from time to time, just in a different way. The sugar skull project was a perfect way to hold family meetings.

Sugar skulls are pieces of art that symbolize a three-day celebration called Dia de los Muertos, the Day of the Dead. Catholics in parts of Mexico, Italy, Spain, and other parts of the world, including Central and South America and the Philippines celebrate All Souls and All Saints Day each year on November 1st and 2nd.

Many believe that the doors of heaven open at midnight on October 31st so the spirits of deceased children are allowed to reunite with their families for 24 hours. On November 2nd, the spirits of the adults come down to enjoy the celebration. These celebrations include brightly decorated sugar skulls, flowers, food, and gifts for the spirits of the deceased.

Italian missionaries brought sugar art to the new world in the 17th century. Sugar skulls signify departed souls. Names of the loved ones in heaven were written across the forehead of the sugar skull and placed on their gravestones. This ritual was to honor the return of their spirit.

By creating sugar skulls with her family, mum was honoring the return of her spirit. Although I doubt this history was absorbed during mum's creative time around the table decorating sugar skulls, I remain certain her goal was achieved. She had a chance to begin bracing the children for her transition to heaven. I know this because shortly after the sugar skull project was complete everyone was much more open about mum's limited time with us. The children began opening sentences with "When gram dies..." and "After gram dies..."

Perhaps this dialogue about cancer and mum's life had nothing to do with the story of the legend of the sugar skull and all to do with time. It took a long time to elaborately paint and embellish several 18 inch molds of plaster.

From start to finish of the project mum had hours and hours with audiences of the grandchildren, my sisters, her husband Doug, and her best friend Linda. During this focused time no one had their head bowed down to their smart phone, iPad, iPod, or tablet. They were painting, gluing, and talking. For the record, the sugar skulls came out beautifully. They are a glorious, colorful, and happy celebration of life and spirit.

Wanda never wanted to hide anything from the children. She never wanted them to be afraid of her death. For mum the subject of dying wasn't taboo, death was a part of the circle of life. To seal this message mum introduced us to the book Water Bugs and Dragonflies by Doris Stickney.

Mum's best friend Linda purchased the book for mum. The book came with a beautiful ornamental dragonfly made of tin. Described as a graceful fable, the book tells the story of a small family of water bugs living below the surface of a very quiet pond.

Once in a while one of the insects climbs up a lily stalk, disappearing from sight, never to return. Everyone left behind wonders what became of them. The answer to their death or disappearance lies in the questioning. The book also includes helpful information about how adults can help children who are coping with death.

"I really hope we can bring the kids here next year," mum said as we concluded our walk through Beacon Hill. Then she stopped in the middle of the street and hugged me. The funny part about this is that I am not much of a hugger. Mum and I had a running joke about this. "Someday you are going to hug me, really, really hug me." She'd say laughing about how little I cared for hugs. "And when you really hug me you cannot say it feels like a bee sting." A bee sting is how I described a hug that lasted longer than five seconds. What can I say? I like personal space.

As we approached my Jeep mum said, "If for some reason I am not here next year, please try to get the kids here to see this." In that instant, we closed the doors on both my Jeep and our time at the other hospital.

We left behind a hospital located at the bottom of Beacon Hill and looked toward The Dana-Farber Cancer Institute, which is located at the top of Mission Hill. In more ways than one we were looking up.

16

Let People In

THE NIGHT BEFORE MEETING HER NEW team at Dana-Farber, mum slept poorly in the hotel. She woke up frustrated. I couldn't help but wonder if we had made the right decision. It was November 1st, All Saints' Day. As we dressed for the appointment I prayed the saints would bring mum peace, that she would bond with her new oncologist and that she wouldn't regret leaving the other hospital.

Boston was a balmy 70 degrees that morning, a highly unusual temperature for November in New England. Flurries of colored leaves were circling all around us. The winds of change were in the air. The Faslodex was taking all of mum's estrogen and leaving her with the cruelest of hot flashes. I remember seeing her beet red skin as we made our way into the hospital. She was visibly uncomfortable but didn't complain. She was focused and ready to take the next step.

Five minutes into the meeting with Dr. Chen I could see that mum liked her. She was smart as a whip, kind, nurturing, and organized. She had a plan of action. Continue the Faslodex and Zometa once a month, reduce the steroids, watch the tumor markers, and rescan in a few months. Dr. Chen's sentences were filled with hope and positive energy.

She parted by saying, "People have success on this medicine. I am seeing people live longer and longer. When it no longer works, we will try another plan. One step at a time. See you in a month." As mum posted pictures of the outside of Dana -Farber announcing her new stomping ground I exhaled a sigh of relief. Operation "Uproot and Replant Cancer Care" was a success. Neither Dr. Chen nor the oncologist at the other hospital ever gave mum a timeline to live. The optimist in me appreciated this. The realist in my mother seemed to want more.

Some days, mum spoke of events in the distant future, other days she questioned whether or not she would live to see the upcoming season of her favorite TV shows. This uncertainty stalked Wanda in the dark, wee hours of the morning. Mum spoke of two voices on her shoulders. When thoughts would creep in about how long she would have with us one voice would say, "Of course you will be here then." The other voice would say, "Who are you kidding? You will be gone by then."

My heart broke the first time I heard mum explain this feeling. Wanda did such a convincing job concealing her worry, most everyone assumed she was fearless. I became obsessed with killing mum's hope-destroying voice of doubt. My weapon was the distraction of adventure.

The days were getting shorter. New England grew dark by 5 p.m. most days. Winter was coming. Gone were the carefree hours spent on mum's deck drinking coffee, smoking cigarettes, painting arts and crafts, eating, and laughing. It was time to up the ante.

Our first move was to book a few days at mum's favorite retreat. The Wentworth by the Sea is located on the island of New Castle in New Hampshire. Overlooking the ocean, the historic elegance of the meticulously maintained hotel was pure medicine for mum. For years we rented the same room on the third floor of the therapeutic getaway. Mum said the best sleep she ever had was at Wentworth.

Mum's Wentworth routine never changed. She would start the trip by over-tipping Ben, her favorite doorman. This practice was followed by greeting everyone in the lobby and remarking on the floral displays peppered throughout the sitting area. From there she would open the doors to the balcony of her room and unpack every single item of her luggage. Once everything was perfectly in place she would stand on the balcony and say, "I love it here. Let's get something to eat. I need coffee."

We would spend hours poking through Portsmouth. As an artist, mum adored the creative vibe and charm of the quaint city. From catching a historic lecture on Richard III, to chatting with a local artist about her jewelry, to eating a croissant while walking by a cluster of musicians playing brass instruments on the sidewalk, a piece of mum's heart was in this seacoast community. With coffee in hand, mum also enjoyed sightseeing as we'd drive up and down the coast of Rye and Hampton. "I could live here," she'd say during every visit. Our jaunts would conclude with room service, TV, reading, and bed.

Since mum's terminal diagnosis I made a sport out of collecting credit card points to gain free rooms at Wentworth. Our goal was to get her there at least once a month for the rest of her life. I watched the site for specials and factored in my AAA discount upon booking. In short, we achieved our goal. Once a month she was able to look forward to a one-night mini-getaway.

She loved deciding who would accompany her each month. "Let's take the grandkids this time," she'd say, planning fun things to do once we arrived. "Let's ask your sisters this time," she'd say, the following month. "Let's ask Linda if she can come back with us next time." Her mind was always planning the next visit. I loved this bright spot on her horizon.

Every other visit or so mum would have a massage at the Wentworth spa. I would hear her tell her story as she walked down the hall to the treatment room with her massage therapist. "I have stage 4 cancer. I am bucket-listing with my family. This is my happy place. You have the best beds here. I sleep like a baby."

One afternoon I found mum sitting in the meditation room following a massage. She was still in her robe, her hair was infused with lavender oil, and she was holding a saucer and a cup filled with coffee. "I am so lucky," she said. "I am the luckiest woman alive. To have been able to have this extra time...to have been able to spend it feeling these incredible moments...to be able to feel this good. I am blessed. Thank you for loving me so much. What did I ever do to deserve so much from all of you?"

I have a photo of mum seated in a cozy chair steps away from the fireplace in the lobby. This was taken shortly after her spa treatment. She looks beautiful and happy. To look at the photo one would never know she was dying. She was too busy living.

If mum hadn't shared her feelings with us we would have never known that she was afraid. I think the life lesson here is to let people in. People usually only see what they want to see. Most of the people around mum saw a beautiful tower of faith and strength. No one else ever saw her vulnerable, victimized, or scared. We are so glad she let us in, so glad she allowed us to see the good, the bad, and the ugly. Through this we learned of the voices on each shoulder. Through this we were able to help silence the bad voice.

When I think about our trips to Wentworth I always remember the moments that took place during the commute home. Inevitably mum would take the pillow and blanket in my Jeep and nap. I knew this was a sign that her mind and body had finally found calm. There was no space inside her head for the hope-destroying voice of doubt. In this brief moment our mission was accomplished.

<u>Wanda Stairs Howard</u> <u>December 19, 2013</u> · <u>New Castle, NH</u> ·

I have to risk being corny but after having a head and foot rub
and then getting this incredible gift for muscles with a heavenly
aroma...I have to tell the world through tear-filled eyes, that
I am truly blessed. My family and friends are the best and if
I didn't live for one more moment...I have lived enough.

17

Find a Space That You Can Call Your Own

*J*UST AS WINTER WAS UPON US mum made the decision to give up driving. She gave her car to her grandson Tyler. She was *so* excited to do this for him. A lifelong lover of driving she said, "God took my desire to drive away from me. As the disease progresses so will my pain meds. I should not drive on pain medication. You guys drive me all of the time now anyway. I want to do this."

This conversation took place after she parked her car right up against the fence of the house one afternoon. A few more inches and she would have hit the fence. This was uncharacteristic of her. As a cancer survivor I know that worry, stress, and lack of sleep can also lead to distractions. It is best to avoid risk before adding high doses of pain meds to the mix.

Although mum never spoke of missing driving there were times when we knew she missed her independence. Every morning mum had a list of things she needed. The list was written on a 3 x 5 note card which sat near the phone in her kitchen. Some days the list read: stamps, slippers, milk, and trash bags. Other days the list would read: face wash, sugar, coffee, dog food, and paper towels.

One may wonder why the list was written daily rather than weekly. The answer is simple - the daily list guaranteed a place to go. The humorous part about the list making is that list or no list we made sure mum was out of the house every single day. I still laugh when I recount the stories of the days when mum wanted a ride to the store but didn't necessarily want a shopping companion "up her ass." Some days she made it clear that she'd be shopping for a bit and that she would call our cells when she needed to reunite with us in the store. Translation: Kindly leave me alone until I am done shopping.

As her lower back and leg pain increased she took to driving around in the electronic store buggies with the basket. God help the person who messed with mum when she was on a mission to cross items off of the all-important list. We have photos of her in various store buggies. Most often she is sporting an unimpressed expression as we snap the photo. I am sure her inner monologue was something along the lines of "Please let me do my thing." I prefer to remember the ear-to-ear smiles she had while speeding up and down the aisles in the buggy. If tickets were ever issued for speeding in markets she most certainly would have had a pile.

Mum loved to pick up little things during the week, a candle here, new body cream there. This desire for harmless retail therapy (we aren't talking big ticket items here) brought us to a very honest conversation one night. As she sat with my sister and I she explained how she was feeling about life.

Although she was grateful for the extra time with us she wasn't feeling as joyful as she had been feeling weeks prior. She was no longer working, no longer driving, and no longer earning money. She had to ask for a new candle, she had to ask for new hand cream, and she had to ask for a ride to get the candle and the cream.

She wasn't complaining. She wasn't feeling sorry for herself. She was simply allowing us in. The cold weather had snuck up on us. Seasonal sadness was knocking on the door. Her husband was laid off for the winter until his construction job resumed in the spring. As with most construction households during lay-off season winter money was perfectly planned for the necessities such as heating oil, the mortgage, utilities, insurance, and food. There wasn't much room in the budget for unnecessary extras. She felt a long cold winter of despair creeping in.

Had she not let us in we would not have been able to design a logical solution. No one dying should ever have to feel this type of despair if it can be avoided. We weren't able to remove the inevitable worry from her mind. We weren't able to tell her when she was going to take her last breath or how the grandchildren would process her loss. We were able to come together as Team Wanda and pool together a little money here and there. This enabled us to remove some of the feelings of financial dependency and desperation.

We set up a weekly allowance and called it Fun Money. Every Friday mum was given an amount of cash in an envelope. The money was to be spent on anything frivolous. She was never to use the money for toilet paper or laundry detergent. The money was for her. The cash was usually handed in a card with a handwritten note validating her worth and thanking her for all she had done for us.

The small amount of money gave her something to look forward to each week. Contemplating what to buy with her fun money provided a bright spot in her brain. As a team we loved offering her this small pocket of happiness. We also came together to augment the amount of quality time we had together at home. My sister declared every single Saturday as family day. She would take the kids to visit mum and would spend the day working on fun projects around the house. Most activities involved paint.

Wanda took to painting everything in sight. She went on You Tube and learned how to transform all of her dark wood, formal-looking furniture into cream-colored Shabby Chic treasures. If not for her failing health she most certainly could have opened a high-end shop somewhere on Cape Cod selling her painted pieces.

Death can bring so much life by destroying the box in which many of us live our lives. Who has ever dreamed of painting their table top and carving the initials of their friends in it? No one in their right mind, right? Well, mum painted and repainted the top of her kitchen table every week. One week it was cream. One week it was purple. One week it was gray. One week she encouraged her best friend Linda to carve her initials in the table. One week she encouraged my sister to paint a table doily in the center. Our mother found great freedom in painting the lines outside of the box.

As the cancer in her tailbone became more painful we removed the stiff wooden chairs in her kitchen and added four padded back and seat chairs with slip covers to her ever-changing, painted table. She purchased two gray chairs and two cream chairs because she was a design rebel. Her furniture did not need to match. She was finished with following the rules.

"Why didn't I replace those chairs sooner?" she said the following morning. "My back feels wonderful. I can sit here all day." The comfort of her new kitchen chairs provided extra hours of coffee drinking, arts and crafts, iPad surfing, eating, and conversation. *Why didn't we replace the chairs sooner?* I thought, imagining how painful it must have been for her to sit up against wood for so many months with cancer eating away at her tailbone. Most days she needed two Lidocaine pain patches stretched across her lower back in order to sit without wincing.

Step by step our mother created a haven of comfort in her home. From the freshly painted, soft and peaceful cream-colored furniture in the living room, to the new dining room table color and cozy cushioned chairs, she moved into her bedroom. She dressed her bed in a duvet boasting sea shells and reef coral in shades of sea foam green and cream. She loved falling asleep and waking up surrounded by the tranquil colors.

Once the house was transformed into a relaxing and comfortable space, we needed a logical solution to provide mum with more alone time in her new sanctuary. Her husband was home for the winter and this amount of togetherness was driving our mother insane. This isn't to say she didn't love and appreciate her husband, she just needed less TV noise and more quiet time. During the very end of our mother's time on earth she hardly ever turned on the TV to watch the news. Other than watching a few shows that she loved, she never wanted to hear the TV.

One night the frustration of cohabitating in small quarters with her spouse came to a head. (Anyone married can appreciate where I am going with this.) Voices were raised, a few things were thrown, and a household object was raised as a potential weapon. Mum's message was loud and clear. She needed more quiet space. Learning of this rumble, Linda and I made our way to the house. It was time to come up with another logical solution.

Cancer hits the entire house like a tornado. Mum needed quiet space to calm her mind. Her husband needed TV to calm his mind. Their home is very small. Although there is a second TV in the guest bedroom, we needed a wider separation. Mum's husband Doug needed a man cave. Their finished cellar (tool area, laundry area, and two small storage rooms) was the perfect way for us to put out this fire.

In less than two hours Linda and I became a design team. We transformed a room in the cellar into a fantastic man cave. We hung all of Doug's baseball hats, sports memorabilia, and Three Stooges stuff on the walls. We set up his fishing poles and reels in a fishing basket. We wrapped strings of white lights around the fishing poles for a soft lamp glow.

We added some floor lighting and a cozy chair and ottoman. We adorned the doorway with his favorite walking stick. We set up an end table near the chair with an ashtray. We even put out a candy dish filled with peanut M&M's. In short: We dedicated an entire room to him. He had a place. In the midst of all of the cancer madness he now had a retreat of his own.

One of my all-time favorite phone conversations with mum took place later on that night. Around midnight she called and whispered so her husband wouldn't hear her. "This is pissa. No...it is EPIC. He is downstairs *loving* his room. The TV must be on, but I can't hear it. I am upstairs on my iPad sitting in my chair. The house is so quiet. Thank God. I was going to have to hurt him if he kept up with the noise of his stupid TV shows. Thank you so much. I am going to go back to enjoying my quiet time. Love you."

Wanda and Doug found solace in each of their retreats for many months. When I repeat this story people almost always admit to feeling annoyed with their spouse. What to watch on TV seems to be one of the biggest disagreements in the home. Wanda asked for help and problems were resolved.

Life lessons...ask for help. Share how you are feeling with people who love you. Open your heart to those who love you. Embrace both the quiet time and the stupid TV shows. Most of all, find a space that you can call your own. Climb into that space and wrap up in warm joy.

Wanda Stairs Howard December 9, 2013

I think it is very healthy to spend time alone. You need to know how to be alone and not be defined by another person. - Oscar Wilde

18

Honesty is the Best Policy

CHRISTMAS WAS DAYS AWAY. ALTHOUGH MUM no longer had the energy to cook her typical Italian feast of chicken cutlets, meatballs, ziti, and eggplant parm, she wanted to host Christmas Eve at her home. Mum's cutlets (painstakingly pounded, paper thin, bathed in an egg wash, coated in breadcrumbs and cheese and fried in oil) were the best I have ever tasted. If we were lucky enough to find a restaurant that served a close runner-up cutlet we analyzed what ingredient was lacking (say for example cheese or salt) then added the ingredient and rejoiced. This Facebook post tells the tale of our true cutlet love.

Lorna Sleeper Brunelle November 6, 2013

The fact that my mother Wanda Stairs Howard just pulled a whole chicken cutlet out of her pocketbook to share with me is one of the many reasons why I love her. #Harvard #Square #Snacks for our Brookline hotel room on the eve of another early morning Dana-Farber visit.

Cutlets or not, mum was hosting Christmas Eve and we were embracing our new normal. We ordered pizza and salad and placed our full focus on something other than food. Time had become paramount. We used our time to play charades for hours. We talked, laughed, and ate pizza until our clothing begged us to put down the crust. This night was unlike any other Christmas Eve we had shared. We didn't shop for days buying the food. We didn't prep and cook the meal for hours. We didn't clean up a huge mess of pots, pans, and plates. We didn't exhaust ourselves in the kitchen. We just sat together and enjoyed our time with mum.

Mum never allowed us to become sad that night or dwell in the inevitable. She kept the laughter going and made it a point to take photos and snuggle with each of the grandchildren. My sister took a video of us playing charades. The video remains on our mother's Facebook wall bookended by holiday messages of love and hope. My niece Paige posted a few sentences about how weird it was to consider that this may be our last Christmas with her gram. I am certain the rest of us were thinking the same thing.

In mum's eyes, Christmas was always about the kids. During the shooting of her legacy video she instructed all of us to make sure Santa always sends his gifts wrapped in Santa Claus paper. This way the children will always know which gifts are from Santa. She repeated this instruction with her eyes firmly fixed on the camera. Her big, beautiful, brown eyes were saying, *"Please keep this tradition alive when I am gone."*

Even though we don't exchange gifts with the adults in our family mum made it a point to sneak each of us a little something. I can hear her saying, "My daughters will always be my children. No matter how old you are...you lived inside of me." She would go on to say, "Christmas is about the kids, but I want to give you all a small gift, because you are still my kids." Try as I may, I cannot remember what she gave me that year. Was it my favorite mascara? A candle? A pedicure gift certificate? This lapse in memory is a sure sign of the overworked mind of a caregiver. All that matters is that our mother was able to gift her children a small token of her love on one of her favorite holidays.

Earlier in the month my mother saw a post about a well-known Boston comedian named Steve Sweeney. After an unexpected opening in his schedule he was looking for a venue to perform at on New Year's Eve. He had done standup at my theatre several times but never on December 31st. Immediately after seeing the post mum called to suggest hosting Steve on New Year's. "Hey, Sweeney is looking for a place on New Year's. How epic would it be to get everyone together to laugh out 2013 and laugh in 2014? We need to laugh. Come on. Call him right now." Within an hour my booking agent sealed the deal. Team Wanda was going to fill the theatre. We had side-splitting belly roars in store.

In the days leading up to our big New Year's Eve comedy show mum developed a cold and sore throat. She refused to stay home so we went shopping for festive party favors. We bought noise makers, 2013 hats and tiaras, beads, and horns. She was excited to begin a new year with everyone she loved, carefree, happy, and laughing.

Moments before we opened the doors to the theatre I placed a Happy New Year tiara on my head. "Don't wear that," mum said as I turned to show her my headpiece. "Why?" I asked. "Because it doesn't look cute. At all." Seeing that I was somewhat deflated by her honesty she went on to say, "Look. You are wearing a gorgeous velvet dress. Your hair looks epic. Your makeup looks great. You are going out on your stage to welcome the crowd in your theatre. The tiara looks bad. It takes away from your look. It minimizes your beauty. You are the host. That's all I'm saying. But do what you want."

I took a look in the mirror and realized she was right. I looked foolish. Beauty was always high on Wanda's priority list. To her there was a difference between feeling festive, looking festive, and trying too hard to sell festive. The velvet dress and high end jewelry said it all. There was no need to dumb down a polished look with a dollar store, cardboard, gold, spray-painted tiara.

This advice was meant to help not hurt me. The closer Wanda came to the end of her life the more honest she became. Tiptoeing around things was never her style but since her terminal diagnosis she worked extra hard at instilling all of her life lessons in us. The latest of her pearls of wisdom was the power of honesty. "I could lie and say the tiara looks cute...but how would that help you?"

The lessons I learned from our mother during that holiday season will stay with me forever. The situation with Doug and the man cave in the cellar taught us that personal, sacred space is imperative. Mum's decision to skip the overtaxing, homemade meal on Christmas Eve taught us that it is okay to simplify and let go of traditions. The conversation about the tiara taught us that it is okay to be honest even if you may temporarily wound someone you love. The decision to schedule a top Boston comic on New Year's Eve taught us that it is okay to laugh our asses off (in public with strangers) while our mother is dying of cancer. Most of all we learned that the greatest gift to give, no matter what season, is time.

Wanda Stairs Howard December 13, 2013

"I may not have gone where I intended to go, but
I think I ended up where I needed to be."
~Douglas Adams The Long Dark Tea-time of the Soul

19

Try Not to Worry

FOR MANY YEARS WANDA LOVED ACTOR/COMEDIAN Lenny Clarke. He is well-known for his role as Uncle Teddy on the former TV series Rescue Me. We decided to surprise mum by booking Lenny at the theatre that January. We laughed out 2013 on New Year's Eve with one of her favorite comics (Steve Sweeney) and wanted to laugh in 2014 that January with another one of her favorites, Lenny.

Mum talked about having the chance to meet Lenny for weeks. Her outfit was selected, her roots were freshly colored, and her accessories were set. All of this was a fabulous distraction from our monthly visit to Dana-Farber. Mum always became agitated the days leading up to her monthly appointments. Lenny Clarke was an awesome, happy event to focus on.

Tumor markers are measurable biochemicals associated with malignancy. It is common for doctors to track the markers. Turns out mum's tumor markers (that had significantly decreased months prior) had climbed back up. We learned this the first week in January when mum's cold, sore throat, and cough escalated. She was short of breath and tired. Because of this, we were seen at Dana-Farber a week earlier than our regularly scheduled visit.

It had been six months since her terminal diagnosis. She pressed her oncologist to rescan and run tests to discover whether or not the Faslodex was still starving the cancer, still buying her time. The bad news: the tumor markers increased. The good news: mum walked up and down the hallway hooked up to a device to mark her quality of breathing. These numbers were good. It was unlikely that fluid had returned to her lung. Still, a boatload of scans and tests were ordered to have a clear indication of why the tumor markers spiked a few hundred points.

As the appointments were being scheduled, the oncologist invited Wanda to schedule the tests at a Dana-Farber satellite hospital. This facility was closer to her home. She assured mum that all of the doctors within the Dana-Farber network are on the same team regardless of location. She indicated that if mum preferred being closer to home at the Dana-Farber on the south shore she would have the option of switching hospitals.

After a thoughtful pause mum admitted that packing a bag and sleeping at the hotel in Boston the night before each treatment was becoming more and more cumbersome. With the freezing cold weather upon us she was no longer able to walk around exploring the city fancy free in her flip flops. It was far less exciting to bundle up and dash from the warmth of the car or hotel room to brave the cold and windy city streets. By eliminating the traffic game we could eliminate the hotel stay.

We saw the decision in her eyes before the words came out of her mouth. "Closer to home makes more sense, especially in the winter. I worry about snow and traveling for treatments. And because you are all the same network we can discuss my treatment plan. I will transfer to the Dana-Farber on the south shore." She would have one more appointment in Boston and then transition to the satellite location.

The comedy show with Lenny Clarke fell between the visit to Dana-Farber Boston and the move to Dana-Farber south. Mum's cold subsided and she was feeling better. We all tried to clear our heads and live in the moment. The scans were a week away.

Mum taught us that worrying about something that may happen in the future robs us of the joy we are supposed to be feeling in the present time. This was one of the hardest lessons. The ability to allow oneself to experience happiness, despite the shadows in the distance, is essential to keep the light of hope from fading. Wanda's positive outlook on life and death burned through our fear like a ray of sunshine. If she was happy we were happy.

If she wasn't worried about scans, we were not allowed to worry about scans. I remember her saying, "So what. We got some potentially bad news. So we aren't going to have any more fun? Seriously? Are we going to be all sad and gloomy? Well, I am not going to allow it." Then in a demanding voice she would say, "We are going to have fun. That's it. End of story. We can't change God's plan no matter how hard we try. So we might as well enjoy every second we can." Under her orders, we put on our mascara and lip gloss and headed in the direction of whatever adventure we could find.

I had heard great things about Lenny Clarke but I knew very little about the person behind the TV personality. My booking agent briefed Lenny on mum's condition. When I met Lenny the first thing he asked about was her. He even remembered her name. "Is Wanda here yet? How is she feeling?" I found myself explaining that she had stage four metastatic breast cancer with limited options for prolonging her life. I told him not to expect to see a sick person. I told him that her outlook on life and her soul were as beautiful as her smile. I thanked him for coming to our theatre.

A few minutes later we brought mum backstage to meet Lenny. He greeted her with a huge hug. "Wanda, Wanda, Wanda, get over here. You look beautiful. How are 'ya feeling? Give me a hug." As he spoke to her he held her hands and looked directly into her eyes. Mum was meeting one of her favorite TV stars. For years she had been his fan. Lenny, a celebrity, was fast becoming Wanda's fan. I have been in show business long enough to know the difference between fake and genuine. Lenny is real and he made a real connection with mum.

Mum and Lenny had both grown up in bordering cities outside of Boston. Mum from Watertown and Lenny from Cambridge, their Boston accents echoed each other. They were one year apart in age.

Lenny had been a comedian and mum had been a lounge singer in the 70's, their paths may have even crossed long before they stood dropping r's from their sentences backstage in my little theatre.

My favorite photo of the night is of mum (a little pint of peanuts standing at five feet tall) looking up at Lenny (a tall drink of water) smiling ear to ear. Once mum went to sit in the crowd Lenny walked over and said, "Wow. She is really something. What a beautiful doll." From there he reached into the pocket of his jeans and took out a gently folded and greatly worn prayer card of St. Jude. He said, "This has gotten me through a lot. For about 30 years I have drawn strength from this. I want Wanda to have it. I mean it. This will help." Before leaving he autographed a picture for me to give mum. He wrote: "To Wanda - Could I love you more? No way! Lenny Clarke"

Wanda Stairs Howard January 2, 2014 · Buzzards Bay, MA

I'm so in love with my latest starfish!

20

Let Kids Paint On Walls

*C*ELEBRITIES WEREN'T THE ONLY PEOPLE SMITTEN with Wanda. She had mastered the art of human connection and could shine in any situation. From the red carpet to an inner city sidewalk, she made friends. I watched her introduce herself to Academy Award winning film actors with the same sense of self as when she obliged homeless people asking to bum cigarettes. No matter what the occasion, she was real.

She wanted her daughters to be real, too. She taught us to love and accept who we are, warts and all. She taught us to be honest. "If there is one thing I won't stand for it is a liar." She said this over and over again during our childhood. Although the root of this lesson started when we were children, (example: "Lorna, did you hit your sister? Tell me the truth.") the value of the message is lifelong.

She concluded these lessons by saying, "No matter what you do, no matter what kind of trouble you may get into, no matter how bad things may seem, I am going to love you anyway, so you might as well tell me the truth." We have a clip of her reiterating this message on the legacy video. I guess she wanted the younger grandchildren to remember this about her.

She challenged us to be free thinkers. She encouraged us to live our lives outside of the box. She wanted us to avoid conformity if it meant feeling more comfortable in our skin. In my late twenties everyone in my circle was celebrating their first and second-year wedding anniversaries by announcing their pregnancies. During conversations I'd mention the names of the girls who had become pregnant. I remember her saying, "Well, this may not be the path for you. And this is okay. What is perfect for some people isn't perfect for others. There is no book that says we all have to walk the same path. Can you imagine how boring life would be if we did?"

While couples our age were painting the kids' rooms in their new homes and apartments, our mother was the one saying, "Let the kids paint on the walls. Let the kids pick the wall color. Let the kids color and draw on the walls. Let the kids hang as many posters as they want. They need to have the freedom to express their thoughts, personality, and creativity. This is when all of that magic is developing." She was very vocal about disliking it when a bedroom for a child looked like a bedroom for an adult.

As an adult I visited the Louisa May Alcott House in Concord, Massachusetts. Mr. Alcott allowed his daughters (who were made famous through the novel Little Women) to sketch on the walls of their bedrooms. The drawings are preserved under glass. All of the Alcott children grew up to be free-thinking women.

Mum was also a magnet for animals, children, and people with special needs. She had a God-given gift when it came to making people feel invincible. One young man named Ben became especially attached to Wanda. Ben is from China and is a student at a boarding school in Massachusetts. The minute he met her he latched onto her. Through his impressive command of the English language he explained that Wanda made his heart feel happier. "Her smile makes me feel like breathing is easier. Her laugh makes me happy. She says kind words to me which makes me feel special and even buys me presents. I think Miss Wanda is an angel sent here by God to bring joy."

During the weeks leading up to mum's scans at Dana-Farber she visited with Ben as often as she could. They would sit on a vintage sofa in my office talking about life, history, music, and art. Some days, mum would bring her puppy Emma Mae to see Ben. Mum believed in the power of pet therapy. We visited the zoo all the time. She taught us to appreciate every single living thing, except bugs. Boy, did she hate bugs. In her opinion, the only bug worth honoring was a ladybug.

A few days before meeting the team at the new Dana-Farber we had to say goodbye to Bruschi, a black and white Boston terrier (named after New England Patriots Linebacker Tedy Bruschi). Bruschi's mother Linda was our mother's best friend. Mum was heartbroken by the loss. She sent all of us a text with the date, time, and place for a Celebration of Life she was hosting in his memory.

She ordered a cake, balloons, and food. She had memory boards with his photos and encouraged all of us to write a message to Bruschi on a balloon. She brought us out to her deck and said a few words and a prayer before we released the balloons. Mum encouraged us to talk about our favorite memories of the sweet dog. She kept saying, "We can remember Bruschi without feeling sad. We can smile and remember how awesome he was. We can be happy knowing he is in heaven with his brother Brady (yes, after Quarterback Tom Brady).

This celebration of life was beautiful. Mum wanted the youngest of her four grandchildren to validate their love of Bruschi through the ceremony. She wanted them to express their feelings about the loss and talk these emotions over with friends and family. She created a safe space for them to work out their pain.

Bruschi's farewell reestablished a dialogue with our mother and the grandchildren about her own death and how she wanted the children to continue to use their words to discuss their emotions and pain. She wanted them to remember how we came together to support each other while remembering Bruschi. I have a photo of her holding and whispering this in the ear of her nine-year-old grandson, my nephew Trey.

The days following Bruschi's return to heaven we met for several movie days at his house with Linda. For hours we would watch movies and TV series with Linda, mum, my sisters, and the kids. Bruschi was no longer sitting on the couch with us, but we felt his spirit in the house, just as we would our mother when it came time for her to join Bruschi in heaven. This was a good lesson for the children to experience. Life goes on after loss. In time, people laugh again and pick up where we left off.

Wanda always loved going to the movies. Aside from the cost of some popcorn, candy, and chips, movie days were pretty darn wallet friendly. We loafed around in our sweat pants and sweatshirts like a bunch of kids at a winter sleep over camp. Time stood still during our movie days.

Just before the scans mum and I met her nephew Jon (my cousin) for lunch. We ate at an awesome Middle Eastern cafe in Providence, Rhode Island, in an artsy community near Brown University. As we were driving away from the restaurant, we saw a wicked cool art exhibit in the middle of a cobblestone patio and a sprawling blackboard covered in white lines with the heading "BEFORE I DIE" stretched some thirty feet across.

This installation was part of a global interactive art project which invites people of all ages to share their hopes, dreams, and aspirations in a public space. Inspired by artist Candy Chang, there are now over 400 re-creations of Before I Die in sixty countries and thirty languages all over the world.

Although we are foodies, this was an entirely new area and restaurant for us. We had absolutely no idea this art installation was on display. Mum always taught us to believe that nothing in life is random. The Italian pronunciation of the word destiny "*destino*" was part of my vocabulary before grammar school. Knowing this moment in time was predestined by God, mum hopped out of the car and headed toward the display.

With the wind chill factor, the temperature outside was in the single digits and we were not dressed for the weather. Be that as it may, mum was going to grab a piece of sidewalk chalk and write her dreams on the board. "Take the chalk. Think about what you really want. What you REALLY want. Then write it on the board. Say a prayer while you do this. This is happening for a reason. We need to really ask ourselves what it is that we want."

The arctic air whirled around our bodies as we became part of living art. The board read:

Before I die I want to: _____.
Participants were encouraged to fill in the blank. First, in purple chalk, mum wrote, "Make as many memories with family as I can." On the next line in green chalk she wrote, "Let all my friends + family how much I love them."

As her naked fingers froze in the brutal cold she mistakenly left out the word *know* as in "Let all my friends + family know how much I love them." At the end of the sentence she added a green heart.

In Hinduism and Buddhism traditions and beliefs, chakras are energy points in the body. The heart chakra is the color green. Despite all of our time at various spas, our mother was unfamiliar with the colors of the chakras. How fitting is it that she picked the green chalk to draw a heart? How fitting that the woman with a heart larger than the ocean would pick the color of the heart chakra to share her dream of making sure her friends and family knew how much love for them was in her heart.

As soon as she finished drawing the heart she turned around smiling at us with a satisfied look in her eyes. "Wait," I said, "I want to get your picture." As I looked at the screen on my cell phone I saw our beautiful mother with her arms wide open. It was as if she was welcoming everyone she loved to see her whole brilliant heart.

Nothing is random. Destino.

Wanda Stairs Howard October 17, 2013 near Buzzards Bay, MA

For some reason this goat loved me. He walked up to me
and just stayed there at the fence letting me pet him (her?)
and then did the most remarkable thing ~ I put my face
near and gestured like I wanted a kiss and he jumped up
and put his nose right through the fence. Goat love.

21

Learn to Let Go

THE MEETING WITH THE NEW ONCOLOGIST at the new location of Dana- Farber was unlike any other experience we had during mum's dance with cancer. Someone called mum's name for vitals and a blood draw. As always, I accompanied her. Blood draws had become more and more difficult and we usually tried to provide comic relief by having one of us go in with her. The phlebotomist made a joke about our neon-colored, matching yellow jackets. Mum explained that we got them on sale before a trip to New Hampshire. "Hey, we love a good sale and we will never get killed in a hunting accident."

Once this was over, a nurse called mum's name. We all stood up to accompany her into the exam room. The nurse stopped us and said, "The doctor just wants to see Wanda. They will talk for a bit and your mother can decide if you are needed after the exam." This shocked us. Since mum's first diagnosis in 2009 we (the note takers, the ones who conveyed information to the family, the ones who reiterated the information to our mother) were part of each exam. We were used to having the doctors pull the curtain in the exam room while we sat on the other side of the curtain waiting to resume our note-taking.

Mum had taken an Ativan to calm her nerves. She had also taken her daily pain medication, and her memory had become foggy. Some days she struggled to retain detailed information. In most medical exams she looks to me for confirmation of dates, symptoms, and her journal notes. "What day last week did I have a wicked bad headache with that awful jaw pain? Remember? The day we iced my jaw? When was my last ankle flare-up? When did you take me to see my rheumatologist?"

I wondered how the heck we were going to advocate for her if we were left in the dark. Rather than project my fear I followed mum's lead. If she turned around, smiled, and said she was okay, I would be okay. If she seemed worried or confused I would make sure we found a way into the room with her. Ever the pro, mum smiled and turned away. We were left behind waiting.

Some 45 annoying minutes later we were invited to join the meeting. A pretty woman in her forties, the doctor told us she had reviewed mum's file and that she and mum had a very honest talk. She said she needed to figure out why mum's tumor markers had gone up. She said they may change the pain medication plan by increasing her dose. She said she ordered tests and scans. Within five minutes we were heading back to the valet.

It was clear our mother loved the independence afforded to her by this new doctor. I remember her saying, "It is so cool that she wanted to meet me alone for the initial meeting. I mean, I rely so much on you guys for these appointments. I mean, I am not saying that I am ungrateful for all you do. It was just awesome to talk to her about what I want, 'ya know? By myself. She gets me now. We have an understanding. She knows I am basically taking this medication to buy a little extra time, to stay alive for my family. She knows I have accepted the inevitable."

For months our mother had Team Wanda by her side. It was never our intention to clip her wings, but on some level we had taken away her ability to fly. This was more than driving her around on her errands. This was more than scheduling her appointments and grocery shopping. This was about suffocating her free will.

Bravo to the new doctor. In under an hour, she handed our mother's autonomy back to her. As worrisome as it was to be shut out from the initial meeting, nothing they discussed needed to be recorded in a journal. Nothing changed the course of her treatment. I needed to understand that sometimes there were things mum needed to say to a doctor that she didn't want me to hear.

Moving forward, by mum's invitation, we were included in every appointment. Meanwhile, we stayed busy with our daily adventures filling the days leading up to the scans. We returned to Newbury Street for pampering and lunch the day before returning to Dana-Farber and mum decided to get a blunt haircut with fresh highlights. We hadn't blocked the appropriate amount of chair time to master such greatness, but stylist Neil made sure he took care of mum. Every now and again the cancer card has a way of bending the rules of protocol.

Within a few hours strands of burgundy hues shone throughout mum's hair. She felt lighter and renewed. The estrogen-blocking medication magnified her hot flashes, so she was happy to get the hair off the back of her neck. I heard Neil speaking to mum about the chipmunk cheeks side effect caused by taking long-term doses of Prednisone known as the Prednisone Puff. He said she was still a knock out. He reminded her that the benefits of the medicine overruled the side effects of the puffy face. A lifelong beauty, she only half agreed.

Our friend Lorraine surprised us at the salon and took us to lunch. We celebrated another cold but sunny day exchanging ideas about enhancing mum's bucket list. A vintage Volkswagen Bus was up for consideration. There was also mention of a road trip to New Orleans.

Mum made casual jokes about speeding up the bucket list. She reminded us that she wouldn't be around forever. We laughed and agreed to kick things into high gear. She liked it when we played along with her method of coping with her death. Tears were never welcome at lunch. Lorraine suggested we revisit one of Wanda's favorite places, Montauk. We laughed about the day we found the Gray Gardens house in East Hampton during the summer of 2010.

The next morning it was evident that none of us had slept well that night before the scans. From July to January I watched with optimism as mum's tumor markers went down. Mum refused to allow these numbers to dictate her emotions. She put very little stock in them. Still, I could tell her energy was jacked up the moment I walked in her house.

Aside from a few bumps in the road with flare-ups, steroid balance, and tweaking pain management, we were making the most of the grace period between the horrible ER chest tube incident and the follow up scans. All things considered, the past six months had been really good.

Familiar with our mother's claustrophobia, Lorraine surprised us the morning of the bone scan. She brought a portable DVD player, a copy of Moonstruck, and ear buds. Wanda loved this movie. Since mum's head was out of the scanning chamber for the majority of the forty five minute test, she was allowed to hear and watch the DVD.

We rubbed her new burgundy head as she listened to the banter between Cher, Olympia Dukakis, and Nicolas Cage. This tailor-made moment of friendship and love made the scan go by faster than Cher and Nicolas Cage's characters fell in love.

Wanda Stairs Howard January 28, 2014 · Buzzards Bay, MA ·

Excited. Going to rent Life is Beautiful and watch it with Elizabeth and Taylor right now. They've never seen it and I love this movie!

22

Make Every Second Count

THE NEXT MORNING MUM'S FACEBOOK WALL was covered with birthday messages to her grandson Tyler. Born on February 1, 1996, he was celebrating his 18th birthday. After giving birth to three daughters and welcoming her granddaughter Paige into the world, Tyler's birth meant at last Wanda had her first boy. We ate cake and ice cream. Mum smiled and enjoyed her time with us. Other than some visible fatigue, one would think she didn't have a care in the world. She was the master of masking fear.

I remember her saying, "What good will worrying do? My scans were done on Friday. I won't have the results until Monday. I have another weekend to enjoy with my family. Do I think about the scan results? Of course. But I can't change anything. This is part of God's plan. Everything will happen the way it is supposed to happen. If I worry now I won't enjoy my time with my grandson on his birthday. Who knows, it may be my last birthday with him. Worrying will ruin my day and I am not going to let that happen."

Her message, albeit admirable, was nearly impossible for me to wrap my brain around. Her clarity nearly took my breath away. "I'm so excited for tomorrow," she went on to say. "We are going to hear that beautiful organ."

As children, our mother took us to the Mapparium in the Back Bay of Boston. It is a three-story tall glass globe of stained glass that is viewed from a bridge through its interior. It is an exhibit in the Mary Baker Eddy Library. The building is connected to The First Church of Christ, Scientist, also known as the Mother Church. It boasts one of the world's largest pipe organs with a total of 13,384 pipes ranging from the size of a pencil to 32 feet in length. Mum's childhood friend is a member of The Mother Church. She invited us to hear the organ during a healing service.

Mary Baker Eddy founded the church to commemorate the word and works of Jesus and to reinstate primitive Christianity and its lost element of healing. Healing was at the forefront of our minds. As Catholics, we didn't care what religion provided our mother with comfort. We were certain the organ music would have restorative benefits.

As we made our way across the church property I remembered a moment that took place months prior. We had spent the day in Boston the day before mum's October treatment and mum's granddaughter Paige (my niece) joined us for some pampering on Newbury Street. We also took Paige to see the table at which President John F. Kennedy proposed to Jackie at the Omni Parker Hotel.

After we left the hotel we drove to The Cheesecake Factory. Across the street from the restaurant we noticed dramatic fountains spraying water into the air. The backdrop was The Mother Church. "We will go back there someday," mum said. "We will show the younger grandkids the Mapparium and walk around, maybe even hear that awesome organ. We will plan that for this spring."

As she spoke we encouraged her to stand in front of the fountains for a picture. Once again I looked at the screen on my cell phone and saw our fabulous mother smiling ear to ear. Her head tilted up toward the sky and her arms stretched as wide as they can reach. The stance of her legs was strong and wide. The position of her hands, feet and head created a five-point image that resembled a star. To date this picture of our mother the star is one of my all-time favorites.

As I continued snapping pictures on my phone I captured another brilliant moment of Wanda. She is dancing as the circular fountain sprays exploded behind her. Wanda always loved the rain. I was thrilled to have a photo of her dancing in the rain. Within minutes she posted our impromptu photo session on Facebook. Beneath the picture of her looking up at the sky mum wrote:

<u>Wanda Stairs Howard October 9, 2013· Boston, Ma</u>

Dancing in the rain! Waterfall?

Fast forward four months, we find ourselves back at The Mother Church. During this visit, the fountains were turned off for the season, but the sun was shining, and we were about to hear one of the largest pipe organs in the western hemisphere.

As we entered the awe-inspiring church, I prayed we would feel God's presence. I prayed he would heal our mother's body and take away her pain. I prayed for a miracle. We heard the organ play a beautiful prelude as people gathered. We heard a gorgeous accompaniment as the soloist sang. We listened to the powerful healing messages of the people speaking. Then, at the final moment of the service, in full volume, we heard the voice of God speaking through the pipes of the organ.

The organist opened up the full capacity of the instrument. We could feel the vibration resonating off of our chests. Overcome with emotion, I couldn't help but notice tears running down the faces of the people sitting around me. The seemingly unworldly sounds coming from the organ reminded me that God's love is greater than mankind's fear.

In this moment I glanced at my mother. Her eyes were sparkling and her smile was filled with joy. She was at peace. This was the moment that I released my fear of saying goodbye. This was when I knew I would be able to survive her death. A wave of relief rolled over me.

As we exited the church mum mentioned the powerful music. She commented on how many educational, artistic, and historic activities are offered in Boston. "We need to do things like this more often. We need to take advantage of everything this city has to offer. I mean, how can you help but feel alive when you experience moments like hearing that organ?"

After church our friend Lorraine prepared us lunch at her home. With full bellies we all curled up on her sofa and watched the movie Life Is Beautiful. This was the second time that winter mum watched this World War II movie that mainly takes place in a concentration camp. On the way home she said, "Didn't you just love that movie?"

After a brief chat about our favorite parts of the film she said, "You see, so many people have had it worse than me. I have lived a long and meaningful life. I have seen my children grow up and I have loved every minute with my grandchildren. No one should feel sorry for me. No one should be heartbroken when I die...because I have really lived. We have to remember to count our blessings and be grateful for all that we have. We have to make every second count. Who am I to ask for more time? Who am I to question God's plan for me?"

Wanda Stairs Howard February 12, 2014 · Buzzards Bay, MA ·

The best things in life are free-
the second best are very expensive - Coco Chanel

23

Quality Matters More Than Quantity

HE MORNING AFTER HEARING THE FABULOUS organ we headed to Dana -Farber to learn the results from mum's scans and tests. During this appointment all of us were invited into her exam room to meet with the doctor. As both a cancer survivor and a caregiver I cannot help but wonder why the heck these meetings don't take place in a more dignified space or at least a space that is more conducive to note-taking, talking, and listening, a space more comfortable for receiving life-altering information.

The doctor started off by saying there was good news and bad news. The good news: In some areas the cancer stayed the same and had not spread or grown. The bad news: In some areas the cancer had spread and grown. Small growth, but new growth. The doctor began to discuss other treatment options. Perhaps chemo? Perhaps a different type of estrogen blocker?

"Why would I try another estrogen blocker if the one I am taking now isn't working? Aren't they all the same?" mum asked. After pushing for a straight answer out of her the doctor said, "Well yes...but..." Just then mum said, "As for the chemo, this isn't going to cure me. It may buy me a little time, but the side effects will decrease my quality of life even more than the estrogen blockers, right?" The doctor's response was vague and seemed to solidify mum's point.

The atmosphere in the room became very tense. I tried to throw out Suzie Cheerleader questions such as "Well, how much time will this buy her?" By "her" I really meant "us". This pissed off mum and annoyed the doctor. Little by little our spirits began to plunge into a dark and deep hole.

The doctor suggested Tamoxifen. This drug was suggested to our mother in 2009 when she first danced with this disease. "You want me to take Tamoxifen now? My other oncologist told me Faslodex was the new Tamoxifen. I have been getting Faslodex injections since July...why on earth would I go backwards in treatment?"

At this point Wanda was crying, shaking, and raising her voice. "You know what?" she said. "I have tried everything the doctors have suggested. Despite the painful flare-ups in my body, I have stayed on the Faslodex to block the estrogen, to starve the cancer, and I have stuck with the Zometa infusions to increase my bone strength. My girls knew that when the day came when treatment was no longer working, no longer buying me quality time, my girls knew that I would end treatment. As far as I am concerned, that day is today."

As much as it hurt to hear the doctor share the test results, it broke my heart to hear our mother say she was done. My heart broke because I knew she was right. To continue any form of treatment would be an invitation to compromise her quality of life. Most of us assume that people would want to fight until the very end of their life to buy more time, but at what cost?

If your extra time is filled with extreme pain, why bother staying awake? If your prolonged days are filled with medically-induced sleep hour after hour, how will you find the time to share it with the people you love? If the medicine used to prolong your life robs you of your ability to eat, how will you have the strength to enjoy the time you have bought? Wanda had considered all of this long before her tumor markers climbed, long before the Faslodex stopped working.

Mum taught us to listen to our hearts. She taught us to respect and love ourselves enough to move away from things that suffocate our joy.

If your boss is mistreating you, find another job. If your boyfriend or girlfriend is unkind, walk away. If your friend is a user or disloyal, stop answering the phone when they call. If college isn't your thing, find a job working with your hands. If depression is holding you hostage, free yourself with therapy and medication. She taught us that when you really love yourself, you know when enough is enough.

Mum had enough Faslodex, enough poking and prodding, enough scans and blood tests, enough appointments with doctors at hospitals, enough painful flare–ups, enough night sweats, and enough Prednisone Puff. She loved herself enough to end treatment, and she knew we loved her enough to understand when enough was enough.

Wanda Stairs Howard February 10, 2014 · Buzzards Bay, MA ·

Every single time I dunk my peanut butter toast into
my coffee, I think of my dad. True story.

24

Embrace Your Inner Child

*V*INCENZO MARIE AKA "VINNY" JOINED TEAM Wanda the next day. Mum hand-picked him with bestie, Linda. Our mother Wanda served as Vinny's aunt. This means she got all of the love without any of the puppy training. Vinny is a Boston terrier. He is the color of Boston cream pie, with shades of cream and milk chocolate. Wanda fell head over heels in love with this pup. Puppy therapy was the perfect alternative therapy for her cancer treatments.

On the subject of treatment, mum decided she would visit Dana-Farber once a month for her Zometa infusion. The cancer was in many of her bones, putting her at risk for a fracture or break. Her thought process was that she was ending treatment to improve her quality of life. The last thing she needed was a broken hip keeping her away from her daily adventures.

The adventures were in full swing. Shortly after meeting Vinny we packed our bags and headed back to The Wentworth by the Sea. The cause for celebration was my 43rd birthday. As I mentioned earlier, the adults in our family hardly ever exchange gifts, we prefer to put full focus on the children. That said, just before we left for our getaway mum handed me a tiny silver box. Inside, resting on a little white cushion, was a beautiful gold heart-shaped locket. Inside were two black and white childhood photos of my mother. "I really hope you like it," she said, "I thought perhaps you could wear it at my funeral."

Although her sentiment wasn't intended to make me sad, I burst into tears as she handed me two other boxes. One box had a similar heart-shaped locket in silver. The other box had a rhinestone covered heart-shaped locket with the word MOM written across the middle. "I want you to have options, depending on what outfit and earrings you are wearing. You have gold, silver, and fancy to choose from."

As I continued my foolish sobbing, my stepfather Doug left the living room and went outside. We were so awesome at adventures, laughing, and cracking jokes about cancer, but we had very little practice crying in front of each other. We reserved the sport of sadness for the privacy of our bathrooms or cars.

Intolerant of my hysteria, mum boldly said, "Stop it! Don't be sad. Especially not on your birthday. We have an epic few days ahead of us. Now knock this off. Take all of this emotion and put it in another place. A happy place. I mean it."

Mom always knows best, so I got my act together and headed toward the hotel. Mum arranged for the room service staff to bring a dessert with a candle to the room. They even sang Happy Birthday. We lounged in our PJ's talking and eating. My battery of my cell phone wouldn't take a charge, and this lapse in connection to the internet kept me focused on my time with mum.

A few days after we returned home it was time for February vacation. Mum loved to keep the grandchildren busy during school vacations. We spent the week in a convoy of vehicles which was usually two or three cars deep. We packed the week with little adventures like a trip to The Christmas Tree Shop where every person had a $10.00 budget to shop, followed by lunch at the Country Buffet. One day we piled into our cars and headed to mum's home city of Watertown, Massachusetts where we visited her favorite Armenian restaurant and market followed by a stroll through the Bath and Body store at the local mall. We got together to watch movies and TV series with the grandkids and dogs wrapped in blankets on the furniture and floor.

Our more extravagant days included swimming and ordering room service at The Wentworth by the Sea. This was our first time procuring two connecting rooms. Mum needed comfort and the Team Wanda travel team was expanding. One room had a king size bed and a deck. The other had two double beds. Each room had a huge bathroom. This was a welcome luxury with our big crowd.

Mum spent time lounging with the kids in the rooms talking about celebrity fashion and school. I noticed she spent extra time recounting her favorite memories with them. "Remember the time we..." or "I loved the day we..." or "When you were little you were the cutest baby." I wish we had thought to record these conversations on one of the many iPads, laptops, tablets, or phones we had in the room.

We concluded our trip with lunch at The Rainforest Cafe. We sipped overpriced smoothies while wearing tree frog paper hats as the room exploded with the sounds of the tropics. Mum would yell, "Look, now the elephant is moving! Check out the monkeys. Here comes the thunder and lightning. EPIC!" Mum always embraced her inner child.

Mum taught us to never lose touch with our childhood self. Following her example, as adults we always colored with the children on the kids menus in restaurants. We always walked the beach looking for shells and always played in the water with the kids while most mothers sat on the shore watching their kids. We went sledding and finger-painted.

We joined the kids in playing with their toys, reading books, and acting out plays and songs. Alongside the children, we believed in magic, Santa, the Easter Bunny, and the Tooth Fairy. We supported the need for mental health days away from school every now and then. We respected the value of an unexpected early dismissal from school followed by an hour at the library or local ice cream shop. Our mother taught us the importance of all of this.

I have the most vivid memory of our mother dressing for a parent teacher conference back in the early 1980's. Although very fashion forward, as a mother of three we usually saw mum in jeans and a cute shirt at home with her impressive hair flowing as her feet with brightly painted toes walked around the house. Parent teacher conference nights were a game changer.

Mum would put hot rollers in her hair and iron her best slacks and shirt. I can see this entire ritual in my mind. On the night of my most vivid memory mum appeared in the kitchen wearing brown fitted slacks, a beige satin blouse, a thin brown belt and a short-waisted, caramel-colored rabbit fur jacket. This must have been one of her power outfits, as she is seen wearing it in many of the special photos taken around this time.

My sisters and I were finishing up dinner when she, freshly coiffed, made her way into the kitchen. All three of us girls looked up at her in awe. She was literally the most beautiful woman I had ever seen. As she placed her pocketbook over her shoulder I was overcome with pride.

I remember thinking that our mother was going to be the prettiest of all the mothers at the conference. She was going to be the Sophia Loren of the entire school. One by one we took turns telling her how pretty she looked. She responded by saying, "If you want to be taken seriously you have to look your best. People decide how they feel about you based on how you look and behave. Your looks matter."

Our mother was the daughter of a Sicilian stunner. Our grandmother Concetta "Connie" won a beauty contest after a ship of Navy men voted on her photo. As legend goes, hundreds of photos were submitted. Connie's sister Rose, our great aunt, was also breathtakingly beautiful.

As we sat at the kitchen table the night of the school conference our mother continued her life lesson about accentuating the positive. "At school, an appointment at the doctor's office, court, the grocery store, the hospital, at work...you must always look your best. You feel a lot better when you look great."

Fast forward a few hours later and our mother could be overheard on the phone speaking to a friend or relative. "I don't care what anyone says, mental health days are important. They are kids for God's sake." Someone (perhaps one of us) may have leaked the truth about us not always being sick on all of our sick days. I can hear it now:

Teacher: "Are you feeling better? You were sick yesterday."

Sibling: "I wasn't sick. I was at the zoo, then we went out for ice cream."

Wanda loved spending time with us. While every other mother did the happy dance each September when the school bus pulled up, our mother was sad to see us go.

And now the time had come for us to prepare to see her go. Knowing that our mother was no longer in cancer treatment we did everything we could to make every moment count, just as she had done for us our entire lives.

<u>Wanda Stairs Howard</u> <u>February 21, 2014</u> ·

I want to thank my daughter for taking us all for a mini vacation in a vacation. I want to thank Linda for coming and always providing good friendship and fun. I also want to thank my grandchildren Taylor and Trey for just being you and most of all God for putting them all in my life.

25

Get Lost in a Good Book

*T*HAT WINTER OUR MOTHER'S FRIEND ROGER Clark had been painting a series of beach houses, lighthouses, and shore scenes. After he completed each painting he would post a picture on Facebook. Every day mum remarked on how much she loved each of the acrylic creations. After reading her comments under one particular painting we decided to surprise her with it.

The painting is a Cape Cod landscape with a tiny, single room house situated in the middle of a sand dune. In the distance the ocean meets the shore. Roger, the artist, had it custom-framed in a frame that resembled driftwood.

Mum's reaction to the painting was even greater than her reaction to the Tieks shoes. She screamed "Oh my God." She held on to each word for seconds. "Ohhhhhhhh myyyyyyy Godddddd!" Once the screaming ended she began to clap. Her teary eyes darted across every inch of the painting, absorbing every fine detail. "He added a starfish to this painting for me!" She threw a playful punch on my forearm as she asked whose creative mind decided to add the sea star. Mum was known to jab anyone in her proximity with a painless punch or slap whenever she became overwhelmed with excitement.

"I need to hang this right now," she said heading toward her nails and hammer. Our mother always had a fully stocked hanging kit at home. Art was her passion. She frequently changed out paintings and pictures on the walls in each room. Seconds later she had rearranged an entire wall in her beach-themed kitchen. The new painting was surrounded by small, square shadowboxes filled with starfish. We have a very cool picture of her admiring her new painting in the wall grouping.

Later that week Lorraine (the girl who brought the DVD of Moonstruck to mum's scan) visited. A lover of art, she noticed mum's new painting minutes after she took off her coat. "This looks like the Outermost House," she said. Having never read the book, Lorraine filled mum in on the story. Naturalist writer Henry Beston published the book in 1928. The book chronicles a season of self-discovery spent living in a 20 x 16 foot beach cottage on the dunes of Cape Cod.

Lorraine was right. The tiny house in the painting resembled The Outermost House. As Lorraine told her more about the story, mum became more interested in reading the book. Lorraine being Lorraine left mum's house and returned a few hours later holding a copy of the book.

Although the blizzard of 1978 washed the original house out to sea, Wanda moved in to The Outermost House moments after she picked up the book. She packed up her life and found solace while staying at the tiny cottage in her mind. "You have to read this book when I am finished with it," she'd say, recounting information from each chapter. "You will love it," she'd say. "How cool would it be to leave everything behind and live in a little house on the ocean? I would love to do this one day."

Hours of introspective reflection at the crossroad between this life and the afterlife had manifested a deep reconnection between Wanda and God. In the quiet moments of contemplation our mother found solace in the words of Henry Beston.

At the same time she was reading the story she was packing up her home. At the end of every visit, she handed my sisters and me a bag or box of her belongings. She kept a log of everything she was going to give away. Every painting, every decoration, every photo, every piece of jewelry, every heirloom was spoken for. Nesting is a term reserved for mothers preparing their homes for newborn babies. Since reading about the Outermost House, our mother had been nesting. She was preparing two homes: one on earth and one in heaven.

Her nesting efforts translated to her Facebook page. During the month of February her wall told the story of her ancestors. Through black and white photos of her childhood we were reacquainted with her parents, grandparents, and everyone else who would be waiting at her new home in heaven.

During this nesting phase she gave away all of the paintings she had done over the years. She even made a point to paint me and my sister Tahlia a new painting for our homes. Each of the paintings was beautifully framed at the local craft store. My painting is of a mother and toddler in a field. They are dressed in Victorian clothing and the mother is holding a parasol.

She painted a scene of shells for my sister Tahlia. "It isn't my best work. I am on a lot of pain meds now and well, let's face it, I had to rush them," is what she said when she presented my painting. She went on to say, "If you don't like it, just keep it in a closet somewhere. When you look at it, remember all of our trips to the museums. Remember what art meant to me. Remember how much I loved to paint. Remember how important it is to have a creative or therapeutic outlet."

During her first experience with breast cancer in 2009 she painted my sister Elizabeth a beautiful scene of a rocking chair on a porch. The porch is connected to a home on the ocean. I suppose she wanted to make sure her other two daughters had a piece of her work.

In addition to the paintings and household items mum was tagging for us, she made sure all three of her girls and all four of her grandchildren had a handwritten note from her. The notes were sealed and placed in envelopes with our names written on them. These final words were placed in her funeral box. No one was allowed to read the letters until after she had left for her new home in heaven.

Part of mum's nesting involved chronicling her life by storytelling. Week by week the list of people who wanted to visit her increased. Her friends arrived with delicious treats in one hand and thoughtful gifts in the other. They spent hours sitting around the kitchen table drinking coffee and talking. I loved the newfound role of hostess, waitress, and busgirl as I tidied up around mum and her fan club. I heard stories I had never heard before as they reminisced about the past or planned adventures for the time she had left with us on earth.

Music was center stage in many of the stories. They spoke about the time "so and so" sang at the club in Boston, or the time that guy was in that band, or the time they saw Tom Jones or Wayne Newton at the Chateau, or the time everyone sang karaoke at that place, or growing up watching Sony and Cher, or singing with her girls all around the house in Belmont, or tucking in her babies during bedtime lullabies. Music, art, food, family, laughter, love, learning, and being a mother *defined* Wanda.

As mum approached the final chapters of The Outermost House she said, "I keep rereading all of the pages I have already read. I think I will put it down for a while. It is so good I do not want to finish it. I just don't want it to end."

<u>Wanda Stairs Howard</u> <u>February 22, 2014</u> ·

I can't express how I feel right now except to say I'm madly in love with this painting, and the fabulous artist who did this special for me...Roger Clark. Thank you. Thank you.

26

Life is Fleeting

MUM SAW THE TEAM AT DANA-FARBER for her infusion. During the visit a volunteer gave her the best hand massage of her life. For real. She looked ten years younger after. I remember mum saying, "See this is one of the many examples of why volunteerism is so important. Don't forget this. Always find time to volunteer. Always find time to help others. This total stranger just transformed my entire day."

Mum met with the social worker during this visit. They talked about how things were going. Mum was no longer in treatment, she was in palliative care. During the visit mum was asked about what role she expected the hospital to play during the duration of her journey. To be clear, our mother's life expectancy was never discussed. We never knew if we were six months, six weeks, or six days away from saying goodbye. None of us ever asked. I guess we never wanted to know.

Wanda didn't want to chase the next clinical trial or chemo cocktail all the way up to her final breath. While some people with terminal cancer will want to try every possible treatment, it's not for everybody and it wasn't for mum. She wasn't going to allow the side effects of medication to diminish her quality of life. She wanted the strength to hug her grandkids and the ability to hold her own fork to feed herself. She wanted to stay awake to visit with her friends. She wanted to be able to dress herself. She knew continuing treatment would lead to what she considered an undignified end.

Having worked in hospice, mum began a conversation about when it would be appropriate for her to transition over to hospice services within her home. I remember the knot in my throat the moment I heard them discussing this next step.

After a brief conversation they agreed there was no reason not to begin home hospice right away. The hospice nurses would stay in touch with mum's oncologist at Dana-Farber. They would be in charge of ordering medication and would stop by weekly to check her vitals and discuss how things were progressing. Our mother was thrilled with the idea of saying goodbye to hospitals.

"This does not mean I am dying right away," she said to us. "It means we have the freedom of enjoying more adventures while I am here. We don't have to be tied down to driving to the hospital and waiting around for appointments. I no longer have to schedule things and find rides and worry about getting up early to be on time for the doctor. I can literally see the hospice nurse in my PJ's." She ended with, "You know me, I am an early bird anyway, but still."

And just like that, our seemingly healthy, terminally ill mother put herself into at-home hospice care. She was proud as punch with her decision. "You wait, this is going to be so much better for all of us." This was about the time the social worker began selling the perks of early hospice care. We learned of the Reiki and massage volunteers who come to the house, and the choirs that sing in your bedroom, and the chaplain who stops by to pray.

Most of all, mum was excited to end the rat race regarding her pain medication. She was growing tired of driving into the hospital to pick up hardcopy scripts for her pain medication and the drama surrounding the communication breakdowns between the front desk, nurses, and doctors managing the refills. Some days we would literally wait three-quarters of an hour for someone to hand us a piece of paper permitting us to fill the much-needed pain medication at the local pharmacy.

Mum filled the days leading up to meeting her hospice team by baking with the grandchildren, watching the TV show, Bates Motel, re-reading The Outermost House, and craving raspberry turnovers. The entire month of March she was happy to eat raspberry turnovers morning, noon, and night. She craved the old school turnovers of her childhood, the kind with coarse granulated sugar resting on a high gloss, half crescent shaped crust. The memory recall of her childhood taste buds was too strong to make do with the modern, puff pastry turnovers. After all a dying woman should be able to have a flaky, crusted turnover. Lucky for her, Linda and I were up for the challenge of baking several experimental batches to feed her unending sweet tooth.

She devoured zeppolis (a decadent Italian pastry with custard and cake) on St. Joseph's Day. We stopped by bakeries to pick some up, and a woman she hardly knew named Judi was kind enough to deliver a dozen to my door for her. The kindness of strangers and friends was in high glory during this time. Daily, mum would open the mail to find letter and treats from people all over the world. One day a box of handmade essential oils from my college roommate Shannon and another day a beach-themed gift from my sister's friend Jen. At the end of each day she knew she was loved.

One night she told us how much strength she drew from the kindness of the people around her. She was convinced her life had mattered. "I never imagined so many people would care this much for me. I must have done something right," she said, opening a starfish bracelet from a friend she made on Facebook but had never met.

She went on to say, "In my generation, it was common for parents *not* to say 'I Love You.' My dad always let me know how much he loved me, but many fathers did not. It is important to tell people how much they mean to you while they are alive. It is important to praise someone when they have done a good job or when you are proud of them. Let people know how you feel before it is too late." She finished this thought by saying, "In my case we know I am dying, of course people are being kind to me, but accidents happen every day. Someone you love may be hit by a bus tomorrow. You won't want to wonder if they knew how much you loved them. Remember this."

It was around this time that our family friend delivered baby Anthony. The hospital was less than five minutes away from our mother, who loved babies. She was happiest when an infant was nestled on her chest with his head tucked under her chin. Just before meeting the baby mum went crazy in the hospital gift shop. She wanted one of everything for him. She also wanted time with him. She secured rides to the hospital and insisted on being dropped off so she could have that time.

The baby arrived via C-section so our mother had a nice stretch of visiting time in the hospital. One day, mum called from the cafeteria. She was buying herself a snack after advocating all morning for the baby's mother because she was unhappy about the level of care she was receiving. "They made her wait too long for pain meds and (yadda, yadda) so she called for a nurse. Bottom line, I fixed it and it won't happen again." Our mother got justice and the situation was under control. People were listening and becoming more attentive because Wanda was on scene.

Our terminally ill mother was back in the game. She was fighting for the rights of our friend, the patient. In this moment mum was no longer a patient, she was the problem solver. From the other end of the cafe phone call I could hear that she was tickled pink with her results. She ended the call with, "They (meaning the staff) know that I am here now...I won't allow anyone to sit in pain...Not on my watch."

A few days after baby Anthony was settled at home we learned of a school of baby Right whales close to the shore of a beach in Dennisport. Located on Cape Cod, this town was less than a half-hour away from mum's house. Lorraine, mum and I hopped in my car and set up shop on a rock with a great view of the whales. For hours we took pictures of the whales and collected shells. The sun was shining and everyone could feel spring pulling back the curtains of winter.

The decision to join hospice and the ability to advocate for our friend in the maternity ward infused mum with a beautiful sense of pride. She was feeling good about herself, and we heard happiness in her laughter. As she sat bundled up on a rock watching the whales she said, "I love this beach. I have always loved these beaches. How sad for the people who work full-time, they can't leave their desk to watch whales swim and play. When they see stories like this on the news they have to drive to work, like I did for so many years. You know what they should do?

They should turn their cars around and head toward the whales. We spend too much time working and not enough time living."

They next day my husband boarded a plane after a conference in Washington D.C., headed home to Massachusetts. When he landed at Logan Airport he received a call no parent should ever hear. My husband's 26-year-old, beautiful son, Brent, had died of an accidental heroin overdose.

This isn't a story about me and my husband. This isn't a story about addiction. Brent was a part of my life for over twenty years. I loved him. He was kind, compassionate, handsome, helpful, smart, creative and loving. He loved camping, off-road riding, fishing and Jeeps. His death has left a hole in our hearts. I am including Brent in this book because the fleetingness of life begs attention.

Brent's short life dramatically solidified Wanda's resolve to make the most of every single day. During the eight months prior to Brent's death our mother prepared us for *her* death. She reminded us that her lessons about life and love should not be shelved until a doctor puts a timeline on your days.

It goes without saying that the loss of Brent was almost unbearable. There wasn't time for me to close the curtains, go back to bed, and put life on hold. We buried Brent on the first day of spring. The next day I drove to Wanda's house to meet her hospice team. I had to focus on the living for what little time I had left with my mother.

Desperate to take action in the fight to raise awareness of addiction, Wanda spent days sending messages to her friends of faith and begged them to join her in prayer. She posted prayer candles on her Facebook and Instagram pages, reminding everyone to stop what they were doing and pray for everyone in pain. "Life is fleeting," she'd say when talking about Brent's death. "We have to make every second count."

Wanda Stairs Howard March 25, 2014 · Instagram ·

On Friday, March 28th at 9 pm please join me in a prayer for help with this heroin crisis that's taken over our country. Too many lives have been taken and I'm hoping the power of prayer can do something, no matter how small. If we all band together and pray at the same time, I just know something good has to happen. If we save one life then it was worth it. Thank you.

27

Hang Out With Happy People

AFTER BRENT'S DEATH, THERE WAS A shift in Wanda's need for serenity. In addition to her search for adventure, she was looking for peace. She loved her time around the table with the hospice chaplain and her dear friend, Pastor Don. The posts on her Facebook page were more poignant and she began cleaning out the clutter in her mind.

Each day she would say, "I really only want to be around people who make me happy. It's that simple. If I don't feel happy around someone, I will not be around them. Life is too short. I *literally* don't have time to feel unhappy." Her decision to shield herself from toxic, negative people or chronic "Debbie Downers" resulted in taking a healthy break from a few of her immediate family members.

"That's it," she would say, "If you make me angry or hurt me to the point of tears, I will not allow you to be a part of what little life I have left. Not going to do it. Not giving you space in my head." Occasionally a few classic Italian one-liners would surface, such as, "I am dying of cancer. You think I should allow the people around me to raise my blood pressure so I can die of a stroke?"

Although this may seem extreme to some, taking a break from the people who wore her down was one of the most important steps she took to keep her energy up. She still loved the people she distanced herself from, but the boundary helped her stay focused on enjoying her remaining time on earth. Grief brings out the best and worst in people. Some people project their grief as anger and others project their grief with grace. Mum's circle became a bit smaller, but it was full of grace, *Amazing* grace.

Mum's decision to join hospice earlier than expected was another home run decision. She had so much more free time and her mind wasn't cluttered with the dates and times of appointments. Our mother really loved her hospice family. During almost every visit she would have us set up a beautiful table of food and snacks for the care providers. She treated them like family and they all seemed to enjoy treating our mother.

During one visit mum excitedly told one of the hospice nurses that her granddaughter Paige was expecting a baby. "Can you believe I am going to be a great-grandmother?" she said, her eyes glowing with excitement. Mum followed up by saying, "That is, of course, if you think I will be around next year to meet the baby." After a painful pause the nurse smiled and said, "Anything is possible Wanda. You are a very strong woman." I heard her pause loud and clear.

This was the first time I realized mum was dying faster than I had expected. There was something about the way the nurse answered her question. I knew the chances of her holding the new baby were unlikely. I suspect the way in which the nurse answered the question motivated Wanda to ask for a T.J. Maxx run.

Retail therapy was still bringing Wanda a lot of joy. As we walked through the beach section of the bargain store she picked up a buoy. "I want to cover my entire fence with buoys. It is going to be epic. I am going to start right now." It was clear Wanda wanted to begin a project that would take a while to complete. Covering her entire fence with buoys wasn't the type of endeavor she could complete in one weekend. "We can get everyone together and drive around looking for buoys. This is going to be so much fun!" Next thing I knew the following post was on Wanda's Facebook page:

Looking for any kind of buoys that you might have hanging
around or if you know of anyone who has some please inbox me.
I would like to hang them on my back fence for a real beachy
feel this summer. I've started my collection and have 2 now.
I know, don't laugh...ya gotta start somewhere right! Lol.
P.S. Of course I'll pick them up.

Mum went into overdrive with her buoy project. We were hitting
every shop in the area looking for buoys for her fence. We even sent
messages to seventy-five of our friends asking if they would like to help
her build her fence of buoys. Shortly after, a public Facebook post on
our walls catapulted her cause.

My friend Lisa runs a non-profit organization named Angels in
America. She collected bags and bags of real buoys from lobstermen
all over the area. Every week mum was able to dump a half-dozen or
more buoys out of a bag onto her deck and sift through her treasures.
She would return home to find buoys left for her on the porch. Slowly
the buoy project morphed into lobster traps and oars showing up at her
home. Little by little every single inch of her fence became covered.
Friends collected buoys from every state in New England. Friends
mailed her buoys from other parts of the United States. Everyone was
part of the adventure.

During April vacation we returned to The Wentworth by the Sea
with the grandkids. We drove through marinas in the area and collected
discarded buoys near or in the trash area. Mum loved the hunt. The
more beat up the buoy the better. If the buoy looked like a Great White
shark had snacked on it for lunch, it had pride of place on her fence.

Mum's husband Doug built her a beach scene in the backyard. He
emptied bags of sand and created a shore with sea grass, lobster traps
and buoys. She put a huge fake lobster inside of the trap. She spent hours
online researching the history of lobster fishing and the structure and
design of lobster traps. She loved explaining the difference between a
wooden frame and a plastic-coated metal frame. She told us about the

rooms of the trap. The kitchen in the trap is where the bait is placed and the parlor is where the lobster becomes trapped.

Mum's buoy project kept us out in the sunshine and gave us a reason to celebrate spring. With spring came Easter. We went a little nutty preparing Easter baskets for everyone in the family. Mum saddled up in the buggy at Walmart and together we filled an entire carriage with treats. As a child mum loved sock monkeys. We found sock monkeys wearing bunny ears dressed in little dresses or suits. She talked me into buying a dozen pink and purple hyacinths to add the color and the smell of spring to the house.

After our rock-star shopping spree the children and adults had fabulous Easter baskets waiting for them at our dinner. We prepared a fabulous meal and covered an entire table with desserts. After dinner we walked down the hill from my home to watch the herring fish climb up the ladder of the river. Every spring this event results in some fantastic photos of our family catching the fish in our hands and gently tossing them back into the water.

This particular Easter Sunday I was focused on capturing a photo of mum with every single member of our family. I have awesome photos of her kissing the kids, her nephew Jon, and his fiancée Karen. Later everyone took turns riding a dirt bike in our yard. We can hear mum's voice laughing hysterically on some of the videos we took on our phones.

Unlike years in the past, when our large family would disperse soon after the meal, this year everyone stayed for hours visiting with mum on my deck, drinking iced coffee and laughing as the kids hunted for eggs in the yard. It was a perfect day.

I heard mum reminding people that she would never be gone for good. She said when her time was up she would find a way to be with all of us forever. She said she would send us signs letting us know she loved us and was still an active part of our journey. She wanted us to understand that we would need to get on with our lives, just as she would need to start her new life in heaven, but that she would never truly *leave* us.

The week after Easter we were invited to visit my friend Jill's farm a few towns away. She had beautiful horses, goats, chickens, and a batch of newly born chickadees. On our way to pick up the grandkids mum began yelling in pain and holding her side. I immediately pulled over and combed through her pocketbook for her meds. "Hurry...hurry," she whispered reserving her air to breathe through the pain. "They told me to expect this. I guess it is finally happening. Oh God. Please hurry."

I tried to remain quiet as she swallowed the pills and continued to breathe through the pain. Tears were streaming down her face, but she wasn't making any sound. Quietly I said, "Is there anything I can do? Can I release your bra in the back? Can I rub your head? What can I do?" She whispered, "Just *please* don't talk."

I watched the clock to report the incident to her hospice nurse. About eight minutes after the spell she said, "You can drive again. I want to try to stand up and see if the pain is there when I stand." "How is the pain now?" I asked. "It is slowly going from a sharp stabbing knife to a dull ache. I am okay. Don't be nervous. Just give me some time for the pain meds to work. Thank God this didn't happen when we had the kids in the car."

About fifteen minutes later all was calm again. Mum got out of the car, smiled widely and said, "See, all better. Nothing to worry about. Now let's get the kids and see those baby chickens." After a few minutes I began to cry. She looked at me and said, "This isn't how we are going to do this. I am relying on you, all of you, to do this with me. We have to be stronger than this. You need to suck it up and develop a thicker skin. Seriously. I am expecting more from you. Knock it off. We aren't ruining the day with tears. We have had an epic week. Remember, sometimes life is hard. *Really hard.* This is when we have to fight *really hard* to stand back up."

At this point mum was on a lot of steroids and pain medication. Her motivational toughen up talks were often aggressive. Although we could hear the steroids speaking through the emotional delivery of her words, we knew her message was always real. Whether in a "roid-rage" or free of meds, Wanda wanted us to be strong. She needed us to be okay when her body finally had enough. She needed us to survive her death.

As planned we went to the farm and loved our time with the animals. There is something about the spring that fills the heart with hope. My hope was that we would find the courage to mirror the extraordinary strength our mother demonstrated during the most unordinary time of her life.

Wanda Stairs Howard April 30, 2014

God sometimes removes people from your life
to protect you. Don't run after them.

28

Look for the Signs

PAIN CRISIS IS THE TERM THE hospice nurse used for the episode that happened in my car the day we went to the farm. Her course of medication was changed. Mum was instructed to take liquid morphine every four hours and Percocet could be used for breakthrough pain as needed. This was another game changer. We were diligent about planning our day trips and always made sure we had enough medication to get us through the next pain crisis. Mum's liver was growing tired and we needed to be one step ahead of the pain.

Shortly after mum's diagnosis she planned her entire funeral and burial arrangements. The plan was to scatter her cremated ashes in her favorite place, most likely an ocean community. She would confirm the location closer to her death. However, little by little, conversations between us indicated that she had changed her mind. One night at a very late (or early morning hour) I received a text message that she wanted to be buried in her home city of Watertown. She selected the same cemetery where her dear friend Jeanne and many of her family members were buried.

The text mentioned her liking the idea of the grandchildren keeping their Watertown city roots alive through visiting the cemetery in the years to come. She wanted us to stop at the local Armenian shops to buy our favorite foods and walk through the very streets we loved as children growing up visiting our grandmother Connie (mum's mother) in the city. The youngest of the four grandchildren referred to Connie as "Grandma Watertown".

The next part of her text was pretty awesome. She asked if I would ever consider being buried with her if we bought a double plot or family plot. I wrote back telling her I would be happy to be her roommate. Badda bing, badda boom, in typical Wanda fashion, she lined up a meeting to chat with the administration staff at the St. Patrick's Cemetery. I'd be lying if I said the meeting wasn't a little sad. I kept my emotions to myself and smiled as she solidified her plans for her resting place.

Wanda was a spiritual woman who believed in the afterlife and heavenly signs. She knew she would be guided to the perfect burial plot and her decision to buried (rather than scattered in the ocean) would become validated. The representative from St. Patrick's sat us down and said, "This is the Saint Jeanne section. Plot 19 is available in row R. It is a lovely area."

The signs were all around us. Mum's friend Jeanne was buried close by; Saint Jeanne. Wanda's father's name was Raymond; row R. As for the plot number 19, both Raymond and Wanda were born on the same day; July 19. Mind you, all of this was discussed in the office before we even saw the location of the plot. The very first plot she was offered was St. Jeanne, Row R, plot 19.

When we drove over to see the plot she literally grabbed my arm in excitement. A statue of the blessed mother and child was in the same row as the open plot. This was always one of Wanda's favorite statues. "This is it! This is it!" she exclaimed. "And look, I can see Jeanne's stone from here." She went on to say, "I am so glad I changed my mind. I love this idea. Just think of the fun day trips you guys will have in the city after you visit my grave. I mean, I know we have a lot more to do in the city before I die, but this is epic."

From there we met with the monument company to select the headstone. Signs followed us around every corner of this part of the experience. We selected the stone in the city of Waltham. Mum was born in Waltham Hospital. As we sat at the desk waiting we noticed the name of the street sign outside which read "Raymond Square." When Wanda read the sign she said, "Hi, dad."

When she mentioned loving Madonna of the Street for an image on the rose quartz headstone the man helping us said that was the exact same image his mother used on her stone. He just happened to have a sketch of the image to show us. Piece by piece everything fell into place perfectly. Mum turned to me and said, "Have you ever had the feeling that something is exactly how it is supposed to be? This is one of those moments. I know this is right. I feel so grateful to have had this opportunity to plan all of this. I am so lucky. I can't wait to take pictures of the stone and show everyone."

Mum filled the final days of April painting almost every piece of furniture in her home. She couldn't get enough of her shabby chic fixation. She, Linda, and my sister Liz would paint and repaint her tabletop. They painted craft store buoys, too. Nothing was safe when mum had a paintbrush in her hand.

The buoys kept piling in from all over the place. Mum's childhood friends, people she had never met, work acquaintances, and Facebook friends had collected well over 200 buoys. Her entire fence was covered. Mum loved sitting on her deck overlooking the colorful buoys. "I love that each one tells a story. Some have braved harsh cold winters. They are resilient like me. Those buoys remind me of my strength. Some were hand-painted by kids. Those buoys make me feel happy. Some were painted by friends. Those buoys make me feel fortunate. This entire project brought so many people together. Isn't it remarkable?"

One night she sat at the table working on a craft project with my sister and her friend Jen. As mum recounted the powerful and overwhelming show of love from everyone who contributed to the buoy project Jen leaned into her ear and said, "What's next Wanda? What do you really want now? What's left?" Without so much as a pause Wanda said, "I want to stay at the Outermost house. I want to stay in a cottage on the ocean on Cape Cod."

Wanda Stairs Howard April 18, 2014 · Buzzards Bay, MA ·

Now I have some buoys from Naples Florida! The shingle is from The Boat House Restaurant. This project is so much fun! Thank you Sharyn. I love you too and can't wait to see you in June.

29

Believe in Miracles

ANYONE WHO HAS EVER DRIVEN TO the tip of Cape Cod to visit Provincetown has driven by Days' Cottages. Known as the Flower Cottages, a long row of 23 darling cottages stretches across the shoreline of Truro. Each cottage is named after a flower. Like our mother, these cottages were rugged. After hurricanes and blizzards, the cottages stood up to Mother Nature. Both had taken some knocks but remained standing.

As soon as Wanda looked at the website she knew she had found her Outermost House. She sent an email saying she liked the idea of staying at the cottage alone but she may not feel safe in the evening. She said she needed solitude during the day. She wanted our company if we would consider not talking much during the day. She wanted to rest. More importantly, she wanted to find the missing piece to her journey. She felt certain something was going to happen while in Truro. She knew everything would become clear and questions would be answered.

I placed a call to the owner of cottages and explained our situation. It turned out they were closed for the season but would reopen on May 1. I secured a reservation for May 4th thru 7th. The name of our cottage was Tulip. Mum, Linda, and I stayed in Tulip and Lorraine stayed in Lilac next door. This particular pocket of time worked out perfectly for the four of us. We planned to return for an additional weekend with the kids and my sisters.

The epic journey to the cottage began with a trip to a local shop called the Brown Jug. We loaded up on fine cheese and cigar-shaped sticks made from the finest Soppressata (Italian dry salami). From there we stopped at Trader Joe's and picked up fresh fruit and veggies for our snacking pleasure. While we were waiting in line at Trader Joe's, the clerk at the checkout asked our mother the occasion for our getaway. Mum recited the short story: Terminally ill, bucket-listing, the Outermost House, Flower Cottages.

Before leaving the parking lot mum walked into a candy shop and spent $50 on candy for the cottage. She was beside herself with excitement. "Wait until you see the epic candy I picked out!" As we loaded the car, the Trader Joe's clerk ran to our mother and handed her a bouquet of fresh flowers. "You are the most inspirational person I have ever met. God bless you." Wanda loved these pure moments of human connection.

She squealed in joy as we approached the cottages. "Epic! Epic! Epic!" She continued screaming as we walked through each adorable room inside; the street-facing bedroom and bath, the side-facing bedroom and kitchen, and the oceanfront-facing sitting area and dining room. We were literally steps away from the ocean. "Do you hear those waves? I cannot wait to fall asleep listening to that sound. Is there anything better than this? How lucky are we? Huh?"

As Linda and I put away the groceries and set up the rooms, mum began unpacking all of her painting supplies. Each cottage had a brick fireplace and guests were encouraged to paint a message on a brick. Some of the messages in our cottage dated back to the 1960's.

We spent most of the day relaxing. Mum painted at the table, walked the beach, ate snacks, read, and became lost in the tranquility of Truro. Although she originally didn't want us to talk during the day she decided that talking was an important part of the experience.

The first night at the cottage we watched the waves change from determined and choppy to serene and still. In the morning we saw the sky switch from deep sapphire to cornflower blue. At sundown we watched as the sky shifted through colors of gold, purple, and pink. Our slice of heaven resembled the painting in mum's home. She had found her Outermost House.

The next day we woke up and sat on the beach. Wanda decided to make a music video. Her concept: Interpretive dance to the song Con Te Partiro - Time to Say Goodbye by Andrea Bocelli and Sara Brightman. She wanted it to be funny, but we had to play it seriously in order to work the comedy. Linda was on camera as Lorraine, mum, and I rehearsed on the beach.

The opening clip was a seashell mum had painted the word Truro on. The fresh flowers from Trader Joe's were placed in a water pitcher on the shore with a few lemons from the kitchen. This was a nod to mum's favorite movie, Cinema Paradiso, as the opening scenes in that movie show a large bowl of lemons on the table. Closer to the water were our three beach chairs, open and empty in a row.

One by one we danced and swayed to the music until all three of us formed a line and made our way down to the chairs. All the while we twirled and overused our arms and hands for drama. Our facial expressions were ridiculously "in the moment." Eventually we made our way to our chairs and sat just as the music ended.

During the rehearsal mum whispered, "I don't know how much more I can do. My feet are really swollen and it is wicked hard to walk in the sand. I hope we can do this in one take." She was too excited to admit that she may have to sit it out. Luckily, we landed a good take and the video was a success. We laughed our asses off as we watched it. Shortly after we uploaded it to Facebook. Imagine our surprise when our walls filled up with people telling us how beautiful and poignant the piece was and how many times they watched it.

That afternoon we went into town for lobster. We spent a few hours driving around Provincetown and Truro in search of buoys and ocean treasures. At dusk we pulled up to a pile of worn out buoys which appeared to be in a discard pile. Impressive stacks of lobster traps provided a picturesque backdrop for mum's bucket list buoy bounty. After selecting two buoys we drove away. Some may refer to our treasure hunting as thievery. We preferred to consider our work a form of recycling.

The next day we sat outside on the beach. I captured a perfectly unplanned picture of mum as she walked up to the cottage from the beach. She is wearing an oversized, lime green sweatshirt and black capri pants. Her hair is pinned up with loose strands framing her face. In the shot her hand is reaching up to adjust the side of her shirt and the blue ocean is behind her. She literally looks like she is floating toward the camera.

Once seated in our chairs, we noticed a red fox running down the shore. We made mention of how odd it was to spot a kit fox during daylight hours. This conversation led us to the iPad to research the fox habitat in Truro. Turns out, on the very same day a fox had been freed in Truro following a paw injury and a rehab stay a few months prior. We jokingly assumed that we had witnessed the first freedom run since the injury. One thing was certain - the fox wanted to be noticed.

Lorraine headed home early to attend an award ceremony while Linda continued to comb the beach for finds. Like a magnet, I felt an urge pulling me back to the storage pile to find our mother a final Truro buoy. I convinced mum, who was both shoeless and braless, to leave her cozy perch on the beach and join me.

We approached the discarded buoy pile. Mum said, "Something doesn't feel right. I don't think we should take one." After deliberating a few seconds longer, I knocked on the door of the house across the street from the lobster pots. If the buoys were not in fact in a trash pile my intention was to make an honest offer to buy one. It was supper time and there were a lot of cars in the yard. In fear of being intrusive, I normally would have returned at a better time. Instead, I lingered at the gate waving to the people inside watching me through the windows.

A kind-faced woman appeared on the porch. "Can I help you?" she asked. After having spent months explaining the buoy project, my response seemed almost by rote. "I'm sorry to bother you. My mother is terminally ill with breast cancer. As part of her end-of-life bucket list she is collecting buoys from all over to cover her fence. We are wondering if we can purchase a buoy from this pile."

A powerful certainty came over the woman's face as she said, "Those buoys belong to my neighbor, and they aren't home. You are more than welcome to come into my yard and take any of our buoys." While we were talking mum got out of the car. With her cane in her hand and her shoes back at the cottage she gingerly made her way barefoot through the yard. As we walked to the side of the house I noticed a few flower beds with Buddhist-style statuary.

Cool evening air was swirling up so I made my way back to the car to grab mum's sweatshirt. Mum and the woman remained near a pile of buoys on the right side of the oceanfront home. It was at this exact moment that God handed Wanda the answer she had been looking for.

To live your life with faith and a spiritual connection is to believe that nothing is random. There are no coincidences. We were about to experience a miracle.

Wanda Stairs Howard April 29, 2014 · Buzzards Bay, MA ·

Sunday night will be the start of My Outermost
House journey. Am I excited? No.

Said no one ever. ⚓

30

Love is Immortal

*S*WEATSHIRT IN HAND, I RETURNED TO the side yard to find Wanda and the woman holding hands and crying. I assumed the tears were motivated by the sacred connection that occurs when the sick and dying and the compassionate and enlightened unite.

The woman encouraged her to select any and all of the buoys that surrounded us. Mum picked up one seafoam green buoy. As they spoke I realized I had missed an integral part of the conversation. Word by word I began piecing together the enormity of the meeting.

I heard the woman say, "She wanted to build a fence and cover it with buoys. She was working on this. We were building this with her and we will finish this for her. You taking this buoy to your home helps me know that she will continue to help people, just like she did on earth. I cannot thank you enough. Now her buoy will be with you for your fence." Then in the familiar voice of an old friend she said, "We are having some pizza would you like to come inside?"

In an almost out-of-body haze I looked around and noticed a partial fence on the back of the property line. I saw supplies to finish the fence next to piles of buoys. The images mirrored mum's backyard buoy project. Someone had passed away before finishing the project. Wanda and this person were both in the middle of their buoy projects. I didn't want to ask the woman to repeat the information she had shared while I retrieved the sweatshirt in the car.

A week prior, when Wanda selected "Our Lady of the Streets Madonna and Child" for the artwork on her headstone, she purchased prayer cards with the same image. A few of the cards were in my car and seemed like a fitting makeshift thank you gift for the lady who shared the precious family buoy.

I handed the woman the prayer card and she turned it over and said, "Isn't this interesting, a prayer of St. Aloysius. Her grandfather's name was Aloysius. You don't hear that name often, do you?" At that moment mum repeated the recent words of her hospice chaplain Rosemary. She said, "She will always be with you. I believe there is a thin veil between heaven and earth. Our loved ones never really leave. She will always be here. She *is* here."

As they stood crying mum asked the woman if she would share the name of the person who died. "Her name is Victoria and I am Ava. Thank you so much for this. Thank you so much for being here. You really have no idea how much this means."

After a final embrace Ava bowed with her palms pressed together. This Namaste farewell sealed the unique connection between two mothers. Before walking away, I took a photo of them. Both have tears in their eyes and look stunned by their chance encounter. Mum is holding her new buoy in one hand and her other hand is holding the hand of her new friend.

Ava watched and waved as we walked back to the Jeep. Once inside mum broke down and shared the intimate conversation that took place when I retrieved the sweatshirt. "Victoria was her daughter. She died today! Her daughter *died* today." As mum continued sobbing I realized it wasn't the anniversary of Victoria's death. She died just a few hours before we arrived.

Through tears mum went on to say, "She answered the door to speak with us on the day her daughter died. Victoria was building a fence to cover with buoys. She didn't get to finish it. Don't you see...the buoy project was never about *me*. It was about Victoria sending her mother a sign on the day she died. She needed to tell her mother that she is always going to be with her and that she is okay. This entire journey- the painting, The Outermost House book, the buoys, this rental in Truro, it was all a way for Victoria to send this sign to Ava through me. This is so much bigger than anything I have ever imagined. She chose me. Now I am completing my buoy project with one of her buoys."

In Wanda's eyes, God confirmed the thin veil through this miracle. I don't know why so close to the end of mum's life she was chosen to deliver Victoria's message to Ava. As an instrument of God, Wanda comforted another mother during an unimaginable time of loss. This miracle validates the unending connection between people who love each other. Our loved ones never leave us. Love is immortal. The bond between a mother and child - a parent and child - can never be broken. As painful as it is to say goodbye to someone we love, we must remember we are only losing their shell. Their soul and love lives on.

Emotionally charged from our meeting with Ava, we headed back to the cottage to share the miracle with Linda. Mum was too amped up to stay put so we drove to a restaurant for dinner. As we got out of the car we noticed a fox (that looked exactly like the fox from the beach) at the edge of the parking lot. Mum stood with her eyes locked on the animal as the fox stoically stared back at her. Was the fox a *wink* from Victoria in heaven?

In China, fox symbolism revolves around the afterlife. Lore has it that a fox sighting is thought to be a signal from the spirits of the deceased. When the fox moved along, we went inside. After a plate of pasta and meatballs mum peacefully said, "I want to go home." She found the answers she had longed for in Truro. That night we cut our stay short, packed up the Jeep and headed home. As we drove away from the cottage she said, "Everything is so clear now."

I believed our mother's journey to the Outermost House was part of her pilgrimage back to heaven. The tiny, ocean-side cottage filled with the sound of waves, and the smell of great food, and the laughter of great friends and family may literally have become the landscape of her heaven.

The night of the May 6 miracle mum said, "I want to climb a mountain and shout this from the top! People need to know that death is not the end. It is not goodbye." By sharing this modern day transfiguration, we are reminded of the sanctity of miracles and the power of love.

Nothing is random. There are no coincidences. Love is eternal. We just have to open up our hearts and minds wide enough to make room for the miracles to move in.

Wanda Stairs Howard May 7, 2014 · Buzzards Bay, MA ·

Friend Forever. Remember that thin veil.

31

Don't Ever Stop Learning

L ATER THAT WEEK MUM CALLED A Provincetown florist and arranged for a potted orchid to be sent to Ava's home. The message on the card sent sympathy for her loss and appreciation for the buoy. A few days later mum sent Ava a letter with a printed copy of the picture of the two of them. She enclosed her address and encouraged Ava to drop her a note or call if ever she wanted to talk.

We approached every single day with mum as a reason to celebrate. On May 8, my sister Elizabeth turned forty. We enjoyed a quiet lunch (and another reason to eat cake) at a local restaurant. While eating boneless buffalo wings, spinach dip, popcorn, and potato skins, mum talked about life. She reflected on her life as our mother. She mentioned how grateful she was to see two of her three girls turn 40. "My daughter is 40 today. Her sister is 43. My other daughter is 34. I look pretty damn good don't I?" she said to the waitress who refilled our popcorn bowl. She finished her testimonial with, "and I have four grandchildren."

The big family birthday party for Liz was taking place three days later on Mother's Day. This day would involve a lot of running around, serving food and cleaning up. It was awesome to slow things down a bit and enjoy this relaxed time together. More and more, I noticed Wanda trying to make time for intimate visits and conversation with the people she loved.

At 6:30 a.m. on Mother's Day mum sent me a text that read, "Let's hit an epic bakery early today. The one I love that isn't too far from here." Within an hour she was in my car and we were off to the Sunrise Bakery, a yummy Portuguese spot in the city of New Bedford. Before leaving her driveway we sat in my car talking. When I asked about her quality of sleep and level of pain she said the liquid morphine and breakthrough Percocet were working well together; she was grateful for the hospice team's decision to change up her meds.

The sky was filled with warm light that shone through the open sunroof of my Jeep. "How lucky are we to have this perfect day?" mum said. "We can bring home some pastry and spend the day on my deck. Maybe cook on the grill. It is going to be awesome." Then she said, "Let's take an epic selfie."

"I am not wearing any makeup. Let's take pictures later when I am showered and dressed," I said. "Let's take a natural, no makeup, 7 a.m. selfie. Who knows, this may be our last Mother's Day. Come on." She said went on to say, "A few pics. For us. Not for Facebook." We leant in smiling, holding our oversized sunglasses as she snapped away on her phone. "Awesome!" she exclaimed. "I love these pics," she said as she reviewed the pictures. "Come on, maybe just a few on Facebook. We look pretty good and besides, who cares?" As she posted the pics to Facebook, I drove to the bakery.

Mum settled into a cozy corner table with a window view while I waited in the long line to place our order. "Let's sit here for a while first and enjoy our snacks and then place the order for home." She was expecting a large crowd at the house. It was clear she wanted to drink in the sunlit seat in the room filled with heavenly smells. "A good bakery always reminds me of my childhood. Growing up in the city, the smell from a bakery on Sunday morning was one of my favorite things. It doesn't get much better than this."

Mum remarked on how pretty everyone looked in their Sunday best as we, without any makeup on, shamelessly ate a corner of just about everything from the display case. She sipped her coffee and chased a warm ham and cheese roll with a petit flan. Custard was one of her all-time favorite desserts. As she watched the people on the street walk by she said, "I have lived a good life. I really have. I hope you all know this. All of you have given me a really awesome life." Standing up to head back in line I said, "We know mum. We know."

While in line I watched Wanda smiling at strangers who entered the bakery. Her eyes lingered on the ladies who were dressed for church. Their bright spring dresses matched the bows which were perfectly placed in the hair of their daughters. The images must have taken her back to the period of dressing her three girls when we were young. Our childhood had such humble beginnings. We were poor in wealth, but rich in love. Little did we know as kids that our mother would build her family and her legacy entirely out of her love.

As I began to clean up the little ledge near our chairs she said, "Wait. Let's just sit here a little longer. We left the house so early. Your sisters and the kids aren't even awake yet. No need to rush. I am loving this coffee." We continued talking and people watching. As women walked by holding stacks of white pastry boxes tied in white string mum said, "We are going to need some of the flan for the house. We have a lot of people stopping by."

Throughout our entire life, all were welcome in Wanda's home. This particular Mother's Day she invited pageant world colleagues of mine, Jack and Doug, for lunch. In quintessential Wanda fashion, she began a relationship with Doug through Facebook. Shortly after she opened space in her heart to add Doug and his husband Jack to her family.

Jack and Doug showered mum in thoughtful gifts. They sat around the table eating and talking as if she had known them her entire life. On this Mother's Day she was sharing motherly love with a beautiful, kind, gay married couple. Although Wanda was always liberal there was a time (many years prior) when she felt conflicted about her faith and gay marriage. To clarify, she was never against civil unions, she just wasn't entirely sure how she felt about gay marriage.

While the boys were on the deck with our family, mum and I had a quiet moment in the kitchen. She said, "I *can't believe* I was ever on the fence about gay marriage. Doug and Jack are awesome. They love each other and are soul mates. Even at my age, even as I approach the end of life, I am still learning. I think God brought them here to remind me that love should have no boundaries. Love...love is what our time here is all about. Who are we to decide who should and who should not be married? This isn't a matter of religion. It is a matter of love and the freedom to love and be loved."

Wanda married her second husband (a Cape Verdian man) in the late 1970's. During that time mixed race marriages were as socially taboo as gay marriages would be in the early 1990's. One thing is for sure, our mother understood discrimination. She understood what it meant to fight for the right to love.

After an epic Mother's Day meal, mum asked all of us to attend a spiritualist church service with her. Her friend Roger had painted murals in the church and she wanted to honor their love of art and their spiritual bond by going to the church.

During the service mum raised her hand for a healing. We sat in a row of chairs while healers prayed over us. I must admit, a tiny part of my soul believed they could make her well. Ever the optimist, I unabashedly asked God to give us more time with her. This was my Mother's Day plea.

The service concluded with a small choir singing an acoustic version of the pop song "Happy" by Pharrell Williams. As we walked to the car mum said, "I loved that final song, Happy. I can't stop singing it." Once we explained that the song had been on the radio for a few weeks she wanted to hear it on our phones. "How perfect is this song?" she asked. "Happy. Happiness and love are really all we need." Shortly after, the song became the ringtone on my sister's phone. Every time her phone rang mum smiled.

The following week we drove to the cemetery to see the headstone. As soon as we got out of the car mum grabbed her cane and cantered to the area of her stone. She was yelling, "I see it! I see it!" I am not going to sugarcoat this - it was very hard for my sister and me to see the stone with her name on it. We couldn't help but wonder how soon the dash after her birth date would have her death date carved on it. At one point my sister became visibly sad. Immediately Wanda said, "Don't be sad. This is awesome! How many people get to see their own grave before they die? Think of how *lucky* I am. How lucky we are to have this time.

Everything is going to be okay." She finished her pep talk by saying, "I am so excited."

From there she began posing around the headstone asking us to take her picture so she could show her friends and family. She stood behind the stone and rested her crossed arms on the top of the rose-colored monument. The warm May breeze blew her bangs and the bright sun illuminated her shiny hair and tan skin. The short sleeves on her shirt framed her colorful end-of-life tattoos.

The artist in her could not refrain from sharing feedback on the artwork. "I should have gone with the Lily of the Valley on the top of the stone, don't ya think? Yeah, it needs a little something on the top. Can we add this? I would love to add the flowers on each side of the Madonna. That would be epic." After years of designing ads in the advertising departments of newspapers, mum was visualizing the graphics for her final piece of work. "Can you call the guy about my stone today and get that done? We need the flowers added before I die."

Wanda was right. This was an occasion to celebrate. The opportunity for her to plan for her dying and her death was a privilege too few are awarded. As her children we needed to honor each and every decision she chose for her death. There was power and strength in these decisions. There would be plenty of time for tears apart but we had limited time for joy together. So, just like that, we flipped off the sorrow switch and began laughing and snapping pics of mum posing at her stone.

At the end of our photo shoot she said, "I feel like a new property owner. This will be my new home. Birds chirping, sunshine, a breeze, Jeanne, my friends close by, I like it here. It's pretty cool."

Wanda Stairs Howard May 8, 2014 · Buzzards Bay, MA ·

I'm amazed every day by the love of my friends and family. Thank you Elle for my huge shell from Hawaii and the sea glass mermaid (2 of my favorite things) mixed together! I know how much you loved her so giving her to me is very special. I love you Elle!

32

Make Time to Play in the Sand

We SCHEDULED OUR SECOND VISIT TO Truro for the third week of May. This time the grandchildren would be in tow and my sisters were encouraged to clear their schedules so we could all be together in mum's newfound paradise. The kids were so excited to spend time on the beach with their grandmother. Mum packed all of her paints and arts and crafts supplies. We spent a lot of time collecting rocks and painting them to gift as paperweights. Mum sat in her beach chair with her grandchildren for hours talking about life. She snuck in every opportunity to remind them of how much she loved them.

We drove into Provincetown and poked through candy and souvenir shops, stopping to take pics of the kids with mum along the way. She was a bit slower on this trip. She needed to rest on benches and stoops in town. She lost some of her stamina, but never lost her energy. She smiled through the fatigue and insisted on moving forward with our daily adventures.

One morning on the beach my nephew Trey hit the jackpot. He found a live, large, chocolate brown starfish. In all my years trolling the beaches on Cape Cod I have never found a starfish. After gently scooping the epic ocean find into his bucket of saltwater, Trey ran to show his gram. Proud as punch he picked up the sea star and handed it to her saying, "Look at what I found! I got you a starfish."

Needless to say Wanda was overcome with excitement. We Google researched the food source for starfish and returned to the shore to find an oyster to slice open for supper. Mum made it clear we would only admire the starfish for a day before returning it to the ocean. That night the kids painted bricks in the cottage. Mum painted a purple brick with a white starfish.

Time stood still during our days in Truro. Every moment was picture perfect. I asked mum if she wanted to check in on Ava. Since she hadn't responded to mum's letter she decided it was best to give her space. "People come into our lives for a reason, a season, or a lifetime," she said. It is possible that I was only meant to meet Ava the day of our miracle. Who knows, we may never see each other again and that is okay."

The next day we drove to the dunes of Race Point Beach in Provincetown. If you are looking at a map of Massachusetts this is the tip of the hook you see darting out into the ocean. Mum's feet and ankles were swollen so it was hard for her to walk in the sand. She took pictures with the kids at the bottom of a dune near the parking lot. She could hear the sounds of her beloved Outermost House book. The piping plovers and the terns were hatching. During each pause in the rhythm of the waves we could hear them chirping in the dunes. Sitting and smiling in the sand she said, "I am always happiest when I am near the ocean."

The last night of our stay, we noticed that mum was a bit disoriented after dinner. She was quiet and more sleepy than usual. She mentioned lying down for a bit. As she walked from the living room to the bedroom she almost fell into the door. She was unsteady on her feet and holding her side. Within seconds we realized she was having another pain crisis.

She rolled on her side and curled her knees up to the middle of her body. She was quietly crying so as not to scare the kids. "Get my pills and my morphine," she said, "hurry." As we brought the meds she said, "Write it down in the notebook. Write down how much I am taking and write the time." Then she said, "Look to see how much I can take. How much did I take last time?"

As I flipped through the pages, my sister made sure the meds got into her. I went into my annoying "fix it" panic mode and began asking what I could do to ease her pain. "Can I rub your feet? Can I gently rub your backside? Make sure you breathe through the pain, Mum, breathe."

She looked at my sister and said, "Please tell her to stop talking. I just need to be still and quiet. It will pass, but I can't talk and I don't want to hear voices. Please." I went to the bathroom and made a cold compress with a facecloth. As mum quietly moaned her way through the pain I rubbed her head with the compress while my sister held her hand. We didn't talk, except to tell the children that grandma was going to be okay, but was working through some pain.

This pain crisis lasted longer than the others before. The cancer was taking over. It was time for stronger meds. Our travels to Truro would be coming to an end. After ten timed minutes of acute pain followed by nearly fifteen minutes of manageable discomfort, our warrior mother got up from the bed to show us she was back on track. "First thing we do when we get home is ask the hospice nurse what the hell is happening. I cannot and will not be in pain." The fixer in me said, "I promise, you won't be in pain. We will stay ahead of this. We just need a more solid plan."

That week Wanda fortified her home with gargoyles at every corner. We searched boutiques in every waterfront community and established quite the collection of gargoyles. Mum named each one and strategically placed them in her yard and in the rooms of her house. In the deep, dark, silent moments of the night mum heard voices of doubt and despair. She wondered if they were the voices of death coming for her. She deemed these thoughts, these voices, as evil. She believed the gargoyles (in combination with her statues of the Blessed Mother Mary) would ward off any evil trying to squelch her faith and positive mindset.

As she placed the smaller gargoyles around the four corners of her house she said, "I will not allow fear to set in at my final hour. I just won't. The nurses will help me manage the pain and these gargoyles will remind me that I am protected. Nothing can hurt me. I am safe. God is with me always." She went on to say, "You know, the meds may start to mess with my mind. You may need to tell me when I seem off. You may need to help me to stay grounded. I don't want my mind to run off with the meds."

We knew exactly what she meant. One of the meds in the hospice life kit we kept in her fridge was an anti-hallucinogenic. One thing was certain-she wanted to be of sound mind. "You know, I may be completely fine right up until I lay down for a nap someday. I may never leave the bed. I have seen this happen in other people. But I don't want to lose my mind and I don't want to be in pain."

The subject of pain was paramount in our minds. The nurse increased the number of times Wanda took her morphine, so the breakthrough Percocet pills were no longer needed. We switched everything over to liquid form. A steady stream of liquid pain meds all day was the new plan. We needed to balance the morphine-induced need to sleep with the need to continue her adventures and quality time with her family, friends, and fans.

By the grace of God mum found relief. In full fashion, she filled her calendar with visits, day trips, and excursions. She continued making daily lists that read, "Butter, trash bags, slippers, shampoo, conditioner, and Tide." She continued her Facebook correspondence with the large community of support who were now part of Team Wanda.

She sat at her kitchen table with us and played with sand. The Paper Store a few miles away was selling jars of sand to allow adults hours of therapeutic play. Wanda loved creating formations with the sand. Her kitchen table became a sandbox. Each person seated around the table played with a ball of sand on a paper plate.

Mum spent Memorial Day weekend on the deck watching her husband Doug mulch the yard with the help of my sister Tahlia, her husband, and the kids. She took great pride in her gardens and was eager to get the yard ready for summer. On the Sunday of that weekend her friend Terry stopped by with a huge box of Portuguese fried dough called malasada.

As big as a hub cap and covered in granulated sugar, this was one of mum's favorite treats. She proudly ate two and half pieces that morning. "These are so good I just can't stop. That's the thing about dying, you no longer care if you are fat. There is great freedom in dying. Just sayin'."

Later that day Linda and I took mum for a jaunt to T.J. Maxx, followed by a Chippi iced coffee. "Epic days. Epic, epic, epic days," she said. "How lucky are we?" She mentioned looking forward to setting up the new dog bed, bowl, and pet accessories she picked up for her fluffy, four-legged bestie, Emma Mae. Once we returned home she stopped by a yard sale in her neighbor's yard and picked up 25 cent gifts for us. She gave me a painted swan and a candy dish. "I could not go wrong! They were a quarter."

On Memorial Day we texted back and forth in the morning. She and Linda had stayed up late playing with sand and talking the night before. She was tired and decided to have a lazy sleep-in day. When I called to check on her Doug said she was sleeping. I sent her a text saying I loved her and would head over if she was up for company. At 10:04 p.m. she woke up and sent me this text, "Just got up to pee. Love you, too. Nice relaxing day."

Wanda Stairs Howard posted this May 1 near Buzzards Bay, MA

So Lorna said let's go for a ride and a bite to eat. Didn't feel great but anything to get out of the house since my dog apparently didn't want me to sleep since she barked at every cat, squirrel and leaf that had the gall to pass by our house. Go to the waterfront of course, and pop in The Sea Witch. Yup you guessed it, gargoyles! She got me a few because she loves me and because the owner kept making deals. That's my story and I'm sticking to it.

33

Break Some Rules

I REMEMBER JUMPING OUT OF A DEEP sleep when my phone rang. It was my stepfather Doug. "Your mother is in a lot of pain." I cut him off by saying, "I am on my way." When I arrived mum was holding her body up by leaning on the kitchen sink. The on-call hospice nurse was seated at the table. She was on the phone going through mum's notebook and glancing at the screen on her laptop. The nurse looked nervous.

"What hurts?" I asked as I gently rubbed her backside. "Right here," motioning toward the upper right portion of her abdomen. "It is a sharp stabbing pain. I can't even sit down. We *have* to make it stop." I asked the nurse to brief me on the amount of meds she had given Wanda since she arrived. She responded by saying that she had given her everything she could and concluded by saying, "nothing is touching it." The pain was finally beyond our control.

I helped mum to the bathroom. She used my body to lean on as she tried to lower herself to the toilet. She spoke in a whisper as she tried to breathe through the pain. "Remember I said I wouldn't live in pain? Remember the promise we made? No pain. I can't stand it. I can't stand the pain." In a very steady voice I said, "Mum, we need to go to the hospital. I need to get you IV medication. We need help. We need bigger guns. The meds we have at home are not working anymore. *Please*, let me help you. This is the only way I can keep my promise."

"No hospitals," she said. "I don't want to go to a hospital. This is why I am in hospice." As I helped her back to the kitchen I asked the nurse if we could go to the hospital for a few hours and return once we got ahead of the pain. I discussed the plan with mum. "I promise I will take you home as soon as we get ahead of the pain," I said. "Okay," she said, "but *please* convince Doug to go to work. It doesn't make sense to have him hanging around the hospital. It is better for him to stay busy. I will see him back at the house later."

When the ambulance arrived, the EMT's explained that mum needed to be strapped to the board or lying flat on the bed in order to be taken out of the house. Mum explained that because of the pain it was impossible for her to lie flat. They continued to explain the policy as mum stood in agony holding the side of her body. In this moment I realized that we were at a dead end. There was no way Wanda was going to allow anyone to strap her down on a table and bounce her around. The EMT said, "I'm sorry, Miss. It is the rule."

This roadblock pushed me into fix-it mode. "Mum, I will gently put you in my car. You can sit upright, and I will drive you to the ER myself. We are going to do this your way. Okay? Who are we to follow all of the rules?" She paused for a while and then said, "Okay."

What happened next was pretty extraordinary. The EMT's and the hospice nurse helped us get mum down the stair and into my Jeep. They encouraged her the entire time with, "You've got this, girl", "Awesome job, Wanda" and "We're almost there." Once we got her in the backseat, I put the blanket I kept in my car around her. As I wrapped her shoulders she said, "Thank you so much. For everything. I mean it. I love you so much."

The hospice nurse followed us and called ahead to form a hospice team at the hospital. I called my sisters and instructed them to meet us at the hospital. Mum continued to breathe through her pain as I crawled, at turtle speed, through the bumpy back roads trying to make my way to the highway. "We've got this mum" I said once the highway was in sight. "We will be there in fifteen minutes."

The familiar faces of our new hospice family were waiting for us at the ER entrance of the hospital. They took turns holding her hands and saying encouraging things like, "Okay sweet girl we are going to end this pain. We are almost there. You are doing awesome," as we removed her from my Jeep and got her into a wheelchair. I took a photo of a beautiful moment when the hospice team surrounded mum. They were propping her body up with their bodies in the one position that felt the least painful. Mum was too weak to sit up, so one woman sat on the hospital bed with her back up against our mother's back, applying pressure to her spine. Two other hospice nurses sat on each side of her pressing their bodies up against her. They were a padded human chair.

My sisters and I kept applying cold compresses to her head, neck, and chest and took turns rubbing her head, hands, and feet. Before long, mum was given IV morphine. An hour into the drip she was still in pain. A doctor came in. He looked through the hospice notes and the hospital chart. He was visibly shocked by the amount of pain medication running through her veins. "I can't believe she is still awake, sitting up in a chair, let alone still feeling pain. We have no choice but to increase the amount of medication. This, of course, will mean that she will become heavily sedated."

Mum understood what he was saying. She needed the pain to end. They increased the morphine. About an hour later I asked about returning home with the IV drip. The nurses began working out the particulars as we texted and called our extended family to fill them in on what was happening. Soon after, a well-dressed hospital employee asked us to take a walk with her.

A few steps away from mum's cubicle she handed us a clipboard and asked us to sign papers. "We know that you want to take your mother home. We just need you to know that your mother may die on the way home from the hospital. She may not survive the ride."

This was the first time any of us realized what was happening. The day before she was eating fried dough on her deck with friends, drinking coffee, and making a list of things she needed to pick up at T.J. Maxx. How on earth could she not survive the ride home? What on earth was happening in her body to rush us into this grave state? I remember asking for some type of explanation, and I remember hearing a vague, "Her liver is loaded with cancer and we suspect her organs are very tired. This type of pain crisis is an indication of everything coming to a head."

In my soul I knew she would survive the ride home. We agreed to sign the release and prepared for her literal and figurative journey back home.

We sat in the hospital room a few hours longer as the nurses lined up the delivery of the hospital bed, oxygen, supplies, a visiting nurse, and, most importantly, an IV line directly into her body, connected to a pain pump for us to press at home. Upright in a chair in the hospital room mum was still but by no means peaceful. Occasionally she would mumble in response to a question. Her eyebrows seemed tense. I kept running my fingers over her forehead trying to ease the tension pulling them together.

Unable to help myself, I asked the nurses the Amateur of the Hour question. "So what happens when we reduce the meds? I mean, what if this was another pain crisis and the pain has since passed?" A hospital nurse looked at me with a cross between a "you poor thing" and a "you dumbass" look in her eyes. "Reducing the medication will mean the return of the pain. She most likely will not regain consciousness."

For ten months Wanda had warned us that the end of her life could be quick. She wasn't the type to spend months at home in her pajama's being sick only to transition to a hospital bed for weeks before saying goodbye. We knew she would try her best to make the most out of every last second of her life. If the day before her pain crisis in the ER was in fact the last day of her active life, she had a banner day.

She ate fried dough and felt the warm sun on the deck. She worked in her yard and enjoyed seeing the yard clean up happening around her. She shopped, sipped iced coffee, strolled through a yard sale, played in sand, and visited with family and friends. This day was filled with laughter and love. This day was a perfect last day.

Wanda spent nearly 40 weeks preparing us for this last day. She directed every step and planned every move that brought us to this moment. All that was left was the physical act of dying. She had provided us with the training we needed to help her cross the finish line. It was time for us to cheer her on as she completed the race.

<u>Wanda Stairs Howard</u> with <u>Trey Mann</u> and
<u>4 others</u> <u>May 26, 2014</u> · <u>Instagram</u> ·

One happy sea star whisperer. @football_trey_mann

34

Do Not Live in Fear

A HOSPITAL VAN TRANSPORTED MUM FROM THE hospital back home. She was able to sit upright in a wheelchair to minimize the discomfort during the ride. She floated in and out of consciousness. By the time we made it home the hospital bed was set up in the spare bedroom, the same exact room mum's father Ray died in after a brief dance with lung cancer.

We lit her favorite Stress Free candle from Bath and Body, cracked the window to allow fresh air into the room, and sat vigil with her as she sat upright in a chair next to the hospital bed. The first few hours were confusing. Mum would jet up to a standing position, as if trying to walk, and from there she would pause, leaning on the person who caught her, until she gently returned to a sitting position. The nurse reminded us that she was on a massive amount of pain medication. We were to expect the unexpected.

The occasional mumbling continued until mum's grandson Tyler walked into the room. As soon as she heard his voice she opened her eyes. With enthusiastic clarity she said, "There's my boy, Tyler!" All of us cheered in response to her lucidity. "Yes, mum. Tyler is here. You are doing awesome. We love you."

Of Wanda's three children I am the least nocturnal. Since living my life without a thyroid I shine the brightest at 6 a.m. and my light begins to fade around 11 p.m. My sisters, my husband, mum's husband, and mum's best friend Linda took the overnight shift. I headed home to build an energy reserve for the long days ahead.

The next morning, we began receiving Facebook condolences. Wanda was known for posting constantly on Facebook and Instagram. Mum's posts and online activity had come to a halt. Additionally, we had called family and a few close friends to let them know mum had been hospitalized. For one reason or another, people were under the assumption that she had died. To avoid further confusion, we decided that I would post Facebook updates about the final phase of mum's journey.

The decision to include mum's Facebook family seemed fitting since she was very open and public about her diagnosis, life lessons, adventures, and transition from the earth back to heaven. Wanda wanted to change the way people deal with death. She wanted to start a dialogue about dying with dignity. What better way to honor her efforts to lift the black cloud that lingers over death and dying than to invite her Facebook friends to hold her hand and walk through the valley of death with her? Here is our first update.

Facebook Post Lorna Sleeper Brunelle *posted to* Wanda Stairs Howard May 28, **2014**

On Tuesday, after many attempts to manage her pain at home, Wanda was taken to the ER of Jordan Hospital. The hospital could not manage her pain without heavily sedating her. Now she is back at home resting comfortably. She is non-responsive for the most part, but we believe she knows she is surrounded by everyone she loves. We are so grateful for your unending love and support.

Once the post was on our Facebook pages, we began to measure the impact mum had on the people outside of our family. We were inundated with messages from people thanking Wanda for the life lessons she taught those who followed her final year. We began reading the messages to our mother as we sat vigil by her side.

Months prior, mum emailed us with a list of things she wanted during the dying phase of her life. She wanted people to read to her. She wanted people to pray with her. She wanted her room to be relatively quiet and peaceful. She wanted anyone who wanted to see her to be welcomed into her home. Reading the Facebook messages aloud to her was one of the first ways we honored that list of wishes.

The next step was to invite people we knew wanted to say goodbye. My sisters and I got on our phones and began lining up the visitors. This portion of the ritual of dying was one of the most beautiful. From lifelong friends to work related acquaintances, the line of people waiting to have a few quiet and sacred moments with Wanda never stopped. Men, covered in tattoos who had fallen on very hard times, kneeled at her bedside holding her hand, praying and thanking her for unconditional love. "She saw my real heart," one man said. "She loved me for who I am. She never ever judged me. I love her for that. She is my family." This man stayed to pray alongside the priest who came to the house.

Another visitor had served some time in jail and was on his way to rebuilding his life. He walked out of her room crying and said, "She wrote to me when I was in prison. She never judged me. She never forgot me. I will never forget this. I love her." One junior high school friend (a Christian Scientist) sang her hymns. One friend (a Baptist) who performed in shows with Wanda sang her church songs. One friend (a Catholic) who met mum through me sang her Edelweiss from The Sound of Music.

Those who couldn't sing read. There was a pile of books in a bag next to her bed. People read her the children's books she loved reading to her grandchildren. Many read passages from The Outermost House. Every hour or so we would read her updated Facebook messages and emails. The common theme: Gratitude for how Wanda welcomed them into her heart and home. She made everyone feel loved. Some thanked her for loving them when, to others, they seemed unlovable.

I mentioned that those who couldn't sing read. This isn't entirely accurate. A volunteer choir came to the home to sing. We didn't know anyone in the choir. Please remember that we are a family of singers. The choir was less than polished. To be brutally honest, they were nowhere near performance ready. During their third or fourth song everyone in the room got a case of giggles. Luckily, they were all standing behind the choir. Shoulders bouncing up and down in an effort to hold in their laughter, one by one they drifted out the room.

I, however, was trapped on a side of the room directly facing the choir. I could neither laugh, nor allow my shoulders to bounce, nor exit the room. I was in their audience until the final note. As their off key, off rhythm sounds filled mum's peaceful space, I began an internal conversation with Wanda. *Mum, I know you can hear every note of this choir. I know you think this is funny. On some level, you probably lined up a few angels to set this up to make us smile. By the way, you are doing such an awesome job. You've got this, mum. You can go whenever you are ready. We love you. Thank you for loving us. They are still singing, mum. Yep. Still singing. For the love of all that is holy, make the singing stop.*

When the choir stopped singing peace was restored in the house. As my husband, sisters, and Linda mastered the medication schedule I typed the next update:

Facebook Post May 29, 2014 · Lorna Sleeper Brunelle *posted to* Wanda Stairs Howard

Update on mum Wanda Stairs Howard - Emma Mae slept with mum all night. We knew that puppy would make her way onto the hospital bed. Mum looks beautiful in her purple nightgown (purple the color of healing) and her skin looks gorgeous. She is breathing peacefully and spent the night with everyone who loves her. Elizabeth read her several books that mum used to read to the grandkids. The Giving Tree - one of mum's favorite books was this morning's read.

Her room is scented with her favorite Bath and Body smell - Stress Free Eucalyptus Spearmint and we keep massaging her hands and feet with the body cream in the same scent. The window is slightly open in her room so mum can hear her beloved birds chirping outside and feel the crisp breeze on her skin.

We are so grateful for this time with mum and thank you all for your love and support.

Team Wanda

The next day our family made the decision to hire an overnight nurse. There were a few moments when mum's breathing was labored and those moments were scary. We couldn't help but wonder what we would do if something else scary happened in the wee hours of the morning. Everyone tried to sleep in shifts. The night nurse would enable Team Wanda's night crew to close their eyes for a longer period of time.

We hired a woman named Veronica. Known as "Roni" she is the sister of our good friend Richard. She was a perfect addition to our team. She read the history of saints and the Bible to Wanda all night long. She even prayed the rosary. Above all, Roni was funny around her. We knew mum loved her personality. She made all of us laugh.

The first night Roni came we sat around mum's kitchen table while Roni had some bonding time alone with mum in the bedroom. Perhaps it was the relief that someone else was on our watch. Whatever it was, we found ourselves laughing hysterically over the silliest memories of mum. We doubled over in laughter, gasping for air, trying not to wet our pants. We made meals out of chips and candy and stayed up like school kids pushing their bed time. One may think our late night party was in poor taste given our mother was transitioning to heaven a few rooms away, but laughter was a huge part of Wanda's life, and we knew she'd rather hear our laughter than our cries.

Team Wanda appointed my husband Roger as team captain during these days. He stepped right up and assumed the responsibility of maintaining the medication log, preparing the medication, and asking the hard questions. He took this off of us so we could concentrate more on what we needed-clear and present brain space to absorb every pure moment while Wanda was still alive.

Although we all still chipped in with the meds, housework, and so on, we focused on every opportunity to do right by the woman who had done so much for us. During her vigil we sought out ways we could bring her comfort. Her body temperature spiked hot throughout the day, so we stored her favorite hand cream in the refrigerator and massaged her arms, legs, hands, and feet with the cool cream. We applied cold compresses behind her knees, around her neck, and on her head. We traced her lips with balm to prevent chapping. We combed her hair and applied pillows between her knees. We told her how beautiful she looked and held her hand. We read stories and thanked her for loving us. Thanks to Roni and our captain we could use all of our energy to help our mother cross over.

Nothing I can write now will capture how I was feeling then. Because of this, I am going to share each Facebook post during her final days with us. The posts begin whenever there is a bold headline.

Facebook Post: May 30, 2014 Friday morning
update on Wanda Stairs Howard

Mum is having another peaceful morning at home. The early sun is shining on her as she rests toes to paw with her puppy Emma Mae. Yesterday was a literal Throwback Thursday for mum. People she has known for the past five years or 59 years visited her. From her bedroom we heard her friends share stories.

Her friend Karen (a like-minded broad with city roots and street smarts) told us about a softball team she and mum were on together some twenty-five years ago. The team raised money to bring the very first mammogram machine to St. Luke's Hospital in Middleboro. Imagine how many lives may have been saved thanks to that equipment.

Mum's friends and family kept up with the housework and made sure the laundry didn't pile up. Wanda loves doing laundry. We recognized the honor of upholding this sacred chore. Her family and friends read to her all day. Many shared a few pages of The Outermost House. Delicious food was delivered by so many great friends. We are grateful for every one of them.

Best of all, our overnight nurse was a rock star! Our confidence in her allowed everyone to catch a few hours of sleep. Before shut eye, we found ourselves seated around mum's kitchen table (between midnight and 1am) laughing hysterically feasting on candy and junk food. We had the makings of an epic 8th grade sleep over. The only thing missing was mum's voice saying, "Enough, it is time to get some rest!"

Mum becomes very warm now. A nurse told us to refrigerate her body cream. We slather her legs and arms with her chilled cream. We have been using her other favorite scent SLEEP by Bath and Body. Her face looks relaxed and peaceful.

I have chosen this photo of mum (belly down in the sand on Cuttyhunk) to go with this post. You'll notice she wrote 2013 in the sand. In July of that year mum was told she was terminally ill. From that point on she lived every moment of every day. She wants all of us to carry on this way. Her example has inspired us to cherish every second.

We know she hears us. We know she will be leaving soon. Her father Ray seems to have already returned from heaven to carry her back home. We had a few signs from him yesterday. We are so grateful for this time.

From the bedside of a cedar wood and chamomile scented Queen,

TEAM WANDA
With Elizabeth, Tahlia, Linda and Doug

Facebook Post May 30 · Midday update on Wanda Stairs Howard

Mum is still resting beautifully. Easy breathing. Seems so cozy in her PJ's. The sound of ocean waves is playing softly on an iPad near her head. Scented candles are in the room and there is a lovely breeze blowing through the windows. Emma Mae remains on vigil at mum's side. Emma's devotion is what inspired the photos I selected for this post. Animals have always loved mum's kind spirit.

Many friends have been reading chapters of her favorite book The Outermost House. Her night nurse Roni Bois prayed the Rosary much of last night and a few friends have been praying with mum today.

Her dear friend sang Hymns to her. The feet and hand massages are unending.

One special part of today's journey - five women, all breast cancer survivors, sat with mum and validated her courage, strength, dignity and grace.

Linda just watered all of mum's gardens and told mum how gorgeous the flowers are today. Her Bleeding Heart is flourishing and two huge purple flowers opened on her climbing Clematis. God is making his presence known through nature. Tahlia and Elizabeth are keeping the house exactly the way mum likes it. #Italian #Clean (we could eat off of the floors)

We know she hears us. We know she loves your kind words. The energy in her room is serene and tranquil. We honestly feel the presence of angels.

Thank you all for holding us in your hearts.

Team Wanda

Facebook Post Lorna Sleeper Brunelle May 30, 2014

We are Wanda Stairs Howard's Audio iPad. We read her Facebook posts every hour. Reciting your love is our sport. TEAM WANDA thanks again. We feel you.

Facebook Post May 31 · Saturday morning
update on Wanda Stairs Howard

Mum had a very peaceful night. On this chilly morning, she is breathing beautifully nestled beneath her soft seashell and starfish blanket. We keep misting the air with the lavender oil mum's hospice nurse made for her. We continue to read her Facebook messages.

We just finished reading her Town Mouse Country Mouse by Jan Brett. When we were kids, mum would sit with us drawing and coloring little animals. She loved illustrations of little woodland creatures. Mum even allowed us to have mice as pets. She named our first mouse Ben.

Ben was our pet when we lived in Belmont - technically making him a Town Mouse. Ben 2 was our pet when we moved to Middleboro - technically making him a Country Mouse. Mothers who say "Yes" at the pet store when children beg for a pet mouse are the coolest!

Love has been on our minds a lot this week. The legacy of love Wanda created has impacted so many people...leaving them changed for the better. Mum's friends continue to sit at her bedside sharing stories of how her love transformed their perspective on the meaning of an authentic life.

I am posting a photo of mum with comedian Lenny Clark today. Meeting Lenny was one of mum's many bucket list items. Lenny was gracious and lovely with Wanda. He spent time with mum before and after the comedy show talking with her about life and love. When they parted, he removed a worn out prayer card of St. Jude from his pocket and encouraged me to remind mum of the power of love and prayer. Lenny signed a photo for mum which reads, "Wanda- Could I Love You More? No way!"

After having only met Wanda one time, he connected with her. The ability to make a lasting impression on people is part of what makes Wanda so special.

I just made the team peanut butter toast. I dropped a slice for mum twice in the toaster because she likes her toast on the darker side. Her piece is heavily buttered and lightly peanut buttered. Just the way she likes it. Someone on the team placed her butter dish in the dishwasher for her. We know how much a dirty butter dish aggravates her.

We wish we could see mum sitting on her deck with her coffee, cigarette and toast. We speak to her about the morning routine so she can envision herself with us buzzing around the house. We still expect to see mum walk into the kitchen headed toward her Keurig. We still check our phones looking for text messages from her.

We try to take comfort in the knowledge that mum lived more in the past year than most people do in a lifetime. Still, we would love more time to love her more here on earth.

This Sunday morning, mum sat on her deck with friends eating warm malasadas. Later that day, she shopped at TJ Maxx and drank a Chippi Mirasol's Cafe. She spent all night with Linda talking and playing with sand from The Paper Store.

On Monday, Memorial Day, mum wanted to have a lazy day. She wasn't in pain; she just wanted to nap and relax. She sent her friends text messages and Facebook inboxes and spoke with us throughout the day. "LOVE YOU MORE" is what she wrote in one of her final text messages.

On Tuesday at 3AM, she woke up in pain and within a few hours became heavily sedated. How blessed is she to have lived every moment right up to the end?

Love you more - epitomizes all that makes Wanda, Wanda and all that makes her legacy of love so pure and perfect. Yesterday an old friend spoke to mum via the speaker phone on my cell. I held the phone to her ear as he said "I love you" over and over again. He thanked mum for making him feel loved.

We will all hold mum's loving spirit in our hearts and draw from her love long after her last earthly breath. Thank you so much wrapping us in your love this week. We send our love back to you.

"Measure your life in love." - Rent

Team Wanda XXOO

Facebook Post May 31 update on Wanda Stairs Howard

Midday update on Wanda Stairs Howard: she has had a few wonderful visitors today. The house is filled with laughter. She remains sleeping and looks beautiful. We just read Love You Forever and will resume reading her Facebook posts. XXOO
Team WANDA

35

Build a Legacy of Love

OVER THE WEEKEND WE CONTINUED WELCOMING anyone who needed a few moments to say goodbye. As each person concluded their visit, we encouraged them to take a buoy from the fence. We encouraged them to use the buoy in their gardens or in their yards to remember our mother.

The support and love we felt was astounding. Friends from all over the country were writing TEAM WANDA in the sand and posting the pics to her Facebook wall. We read every message to her. Other than one moment when a hospice nurse insisted on trying to rotate our mother's sleeping position (which caused some labored respiratory sounds) she remained still, peaceful, and beautiful.

As a team we decided against any further hospice recommendations to turn our mother. One of the CNAs told us a lot of people die in hospice as they are being turned. No sooner than I heard her mention this, I began texting my friends in the nursing profession. Within ten minutes, three nurses wrote back confirming the information about turning terminal patients days away from death. We all agreed that we had come too far in her journey to have it end in such an undignified way. Our mother was in the process of dying...why on earth would it matter if we rotated her body to prevent bed sores?

On Sunday, June 1st, I lifted the May page of the wall calendar in the hall just off of mum's kitchen. I wanted to see if there were any appointments we needed to cancel. June 1st had the word "TRURO" written on it. We were due to check in to her cottage by the sea any time after 3 p.m. "Don't be surprised if she dies today," I said to my sisters. "Once she is packed and ready for Truro or any trip, nothing will stop her. If she dies today, she will be able to fly to Truro." Knowing our mother, we all agreed she never missed the opportunity for a trip. While most everyone we know was waking up that morning, I wrote the following post:

Facebook Post Sunday, June 1st morning
update on Wanda Stairs Howard

"People sometimes ask if it was hard being a young mother. I always tell them that all of my life I wanted to be a mother. I just always knew that is what I wanted to be. Well, that and a school teacher or a nun... but always a mother. My entire life my kids have been everything. I used to be sad every September when they had to go back to school. I just loved being with them. So no...I never thought it was hard to be a young mother. Motherhood was all I ever wanted and I had the chance to have it." -Wanda Howard

Mum had a restful and peaceful night. Our fabulous night nurse Roni read to her for hours. One of mum's favorite topics - the history of saints. The house smells of coffee, lavender and patchouli. Some of mum's favorite scents.

People mum holds dear in her heart visited yesterday and sat by her bedside holding her hand and reading to her. One friend said, "Wanda always sees the good in everyone. She sees their real heart. She sees beneath the exterior. This is what makes her so beautiful."

Many people have mentioned that Wanda is the mother they always wanted. Many of our childhood friends say, as kids, they loved being at our house and wanted to move in. They all agree the most important ingredient in mum's mothering recipe for success was love. Mum had enough love for every child in the neighborhood, and that included every one of our friends.

Wanda's beauty was a common theme yesterday. Everyone remarked on how stunning she was in life and is still near death. They all agreed her happy, show stopping smile is contagious. Her hair was also pretty epic. Mum credits quality hair products for her styling success.

We always knew we were mum's first and only priority. A lioness, she had our backs no matter what type of situation we landed. Loyalty is paramount in our household and family always comes first. We love this about her. These principals are apparent in our devotion to her.

As a grandmother she immersed herself in the second generation of her babies. Her happiest times were spent with the grandkids, in a creative environment, learning about or doing something cool and interesting. As a result, her grandkids can identify several types of birds by name. Mum takes great pride in this.

We know mum hears us. We continue to read her Facebook posts. We continue to thank her for loving us, sacrificing for us, advocating for us, singing to us, reading to us, cooking beautiful meals for us and teaching us how to be good people.

We continue to tell her that her father Ray and her brother Ray are here and that it is okay for her to go back home to heaven with them. We continue to remind her that all she ever wanted to be is a mother and that she achieved and mastered her most important wish.

Mum was supposed return to "her" cottage in Truro today for a few days. We keep telling her to go to the ocean and smell the salty air. We pray the angels will lift her up to fly down the shore.

Mother, teacher or nun... two out of three ain't bad. Besides, she was way too stylish to rock those comfortable nun shoes!

We love you all-

TEAM WANDA

Facebook Post Lorna Sleeper Brunelle June 1, 2014
· Midday update on Wanda Stairs Howard

Mum has had a very quiet afternoon. We are still reading to her, massaging her feet and hands with her favorite cream and sharing our favorite memories. Mum loves this type of relaxing Sunday. Her energy feels very happy.

Thanks for your continued love.
Team Wanda

<u>Facebook Post Lorna Sleeper Brunelle June 1, 2014</u>

Sitting next to Wanda Stairs Howard (AKA Sleeping Beauty) reflecting on what a remarkable journey she has had.

36

Tell Someone You Love Them

$\mathcal{I}$ SPENT MOST OF JUNE 1ST TAKING pictures of mum with our immediate family. I had documented every step of her journey and wanted to be sure to remember this, the final stage. I have one especially stunning photo of my sister Liz taking a nap in the chair next to the hospital bed. She fell asleep holding mum's hand.

I have another poignant set of photos of my sister Tahlia and mum's friend Linda each lying in the hospital bed with mum. In one of these pictures, mum's husband Doug is sitting in the chair next to her bed. If you look beyond the exhaustion and sadness you can see a sense of peace in every photo. We knew we had done our job. We had honored her life by bringing dignity to her death.

In the late evening, Liz continued to read "The Outermost House" aloud while Linda rubbed Wanda's head. Wanda never wanted the story to end. She would read the book, get to the final chapter and then flip the pages back to the beginning. Wanda was so in love with the imagery of the story, she didn't want to give it up. Just as Liz was approaching the final ten pages of the book, she and Linda noticed a change in Wanda's breathing. There was a significant delay in between each breath. After the second long and delayed pause in Wanda's breathing, Liz went to find our captain Roger.

I remember hearing my husband say, "Hey hun, I think it's time." From there Tahlia, Tyler, Doug and everyone in the house gathered, and we made a complete circle around mum's hospital bed. Every one of us held onto a part of her body. I leaned my body against her back. We literally cheered for her as we felt her crossing the line between earth and heaven. "You can do it, mum!" we said, "You are doing awesome. Go mum, go! You've got this. Grandpa G.G. is waiting for you. You are doing it, mum! You are almost there. Fly to the beach. Do you see Truro? Fly mum. Fly! We are going to hug you all the way to heaven. You've got this and we've got you."

Every one of us held onto her. There wasn't a part of her body that wasn't surrounded by Team Wanda, surrounded by love. The final physical act of dying is quick, but time seemed to stop as we guided her through the last moments in her body. Life was suspended, nothing felt rushed.

I remember hearing my sister Liz say, "You are doing *so* awesome. Good job, mum. You are almost there." As her body began to gently quiver we all began saying, "I love you." I held on to her right leg and leaned my body on the back side of her body. I repeated, "Thank you, mum. I love you. Thank you." until the quivering stopped. Team Wanda continued to coach her to heaven until we heard her last breath. She wasn't in pain. She was peaceful and surrounded by love. In this astonishing moment, her beautiful life on earth ended as her beautiful life in heaven began.

At the *exact* second she left us, we heard the song "Happy" playing loudly in the room. It was the ringtone of Liz's phone. Liz was visibly upset by the call. In an effort to shut off her ringer she said, "You've got to be kidding me. Can someone hand me my phone?" Less than five minutes earlier, Liz's daughter Paige headed home to rest. Paige was calling Liz to answer a question Liz had left on a voicemail for Paige.

As the ringtone "Happy" continued to play I said, "Liz, wait a minute. Remember mum said she would send us a sign right away? *This* is the sign. The moment she took her last breath, the song "Happy" came on. She is happy. Get it? It is so typical of mum to use Paige to tell us she is okay. She planned it this way. This is the part Paige was supposed to play in mum's final chapter. Now we know she is happy."

As for the final chapter, it was clear Wanda didn't want Liz to finish the "Outermost House." She transitioned to heaven before Liz could get to the end. Mum always said the journey was more important than the destination. Perhaps she was reminding all of us to enjoy the ride.

Despite the undeniably awesome sign that Wanda was happy, we couldn't deny the immediate pain of losing her. While a tearful Team Wanda began to disperse in the house with their spouses and children, I remained in the room with mum. Having not cried in front of her all week, I rested my upper body on the end of mum's bed and sobbed and wailed. Her perfectly manicured toes and pretty feet reminded me of how quickly she went from living a full life to dying. Days before her pain crisis we sat side by side in pedicure chairs. How on earth could she already be gone?

Wanda wouldn't approve of all of the tears. She'd want us to begin making the calls and gathering the family. We invited my cousin Jon and a few people who had left the house just before she died to come back and sit with Wanda before she was taken to the funeral home. Once hospice was called, we took turns having quiet time with Wanda as we waited for them to arrive.

The two youngest of the four grandchildren wanted to be sure she looked really nice when she left for the funeral home. They got her makeup bag out of her pocketbook and applied lip gloss to her lips. "Gram would want to look awesome," my niece Taylor said. My nephew Trey followed up with "Yeah, she likes this lip gloss." I took pictures of mum's lip gloss wearing body. It is a gorgeously raw image I don't ever want to forget.

Shortly after hospice and the funeral home staff arrived the subject of getting Wanda through the house and into the hearse was discussed. There would be no zipping of a body bag and no full body swaddle wrapping in a sheet. Death with dignity means a stunning, Queen-like final exit from your home.

To avoid the unattractive moments of wheeling her through the house, my husband initiated the idea of a parade. Team Wanda would line up in the driveway and wait to cheer her on. Meanwhile, she would remain visible from the waist up, the lower half of her body would be swaddled in a pretty quilt and her head would rest high on extra pillows. Close to twenty people lined her driveway waiting. We played the song "Happy" on one of our phones. Shortly after the music began to play we saw our beautiful mother make her way down the parade route.

The moment we saw her we began clapping. The applause continued as we began shouting, "You did it! You are awesome. WE LOVE YOU! You look beautiful. Thank you!" The porch light and the street light shone down on her like spotlights. The position of her mouth from resting on her side for a few days looked like a smile to anyone who cheered on the left side of the parade route. "Look, she is smiling!" I announced as we continued clapping. "She loves this!"

The applause, the "Happy" song, and the words of encouragement were equally as awesome as the look on the faces of the staff from the funeral home. Unbeknownst to them, they were the unsuspecting drivers of mum's float in the parade. Needless to say, they seemed awkwardly impressed by our celebration of life antics. One particular man from the funeral home smiled at me as if to say, "This is so awesome."

Team Wanda flooded the back of the hearse as they glided Wanda into the vehicle. "We love you. Team Wanda loves you. You did it!" We continued clapping until the hearse pulled around the street. Once they were out of view, we gathered around mum's buoy fence and took a Team Wanda photo and a few Team Wanda selfies.

I walked out on the deck that brought Wanda so much joy and looked up at a sky filled with stars. *You did it, mum. You did it. I miss you so much already.*

Facebook Post June 1 · *posted to* Wanda Stairs Howard

Dear Friends,

At 8:53PM tonight Wanda became an angel. Elizabeth was reading her The Outermost House and her family, Linda and puppy Emma Mae surrounded her bed.

We all held on to her and said, "We are going to hug you all the way to heaven! Go ahead, mum...you've got this and we've got you. Be with Grandpa G.G." As we heard her last breath, a phone rang. The ringtone was Pharrell's "Happy." Immediately, we knew mum was HAPPY! We felt her spirit dancing. Although mum is permitting us to be "sad for one day" we felt her lift us up.

Wanda's transition to heaven was one of the most beautiful things we have ever seen. We thanked mum for sharing her final moments on earth with us and congratulated her on a most beautiful send off.

We are now planning to line up, clap and play music as she is escorted to her chariot. The grandkids are putting her favorite lipstick on her.

Join us in the celebration of her life by taking the time to tell someone you love them.

Thank you all for all of the love!
XXOO Team Wanda

37

Be Grateful

WANDA DIED ON JUNE 1ST EXACTLY five years after the date of her first surgery for breast cancer in 2009. Many people with cancer consider their surgeryversary to be their rebirth day. On Wanda's rebirth day she was able to celebrate in heaven with the people she had missed for many years. The rebirth cake must have been a rum cake filled with custard and covered in cream and fresh strawberries. Mum wouldn't have it any other way.

Facebook Post Lorna Sleeper Brunelle June 2, 2014

I woke up remembering that we kind of had a parade for Wanda Stairs Howard in her driveway last night. How cool was that? Did you see her smiling? The dudes from the funeral home were smiling, too.
#Dignity #Queen
TEAM WANDA

The next morning Team Wanda went to mum's favorite nail salon. We all got manicures and pedicures. Each of us had one finger and one toe decorated with a starfish. Prior to this I was a nail art virgin. I was overcome by the messages from people who said our daily posts on mum's journey changed the way they thought about death and dying. Many asked if they could continue to be included in our journey through the day of her burial. For Wanda who so desperately wanted to change the way people view death and for her Facebook friends, I kept posting. Here are the June 2nd posts.

June 2 · Lorna Sleeper Brunelle

June 1st marks the start of Meteorological Summer. Mum Wanda Stairs Howard turned her wall calendar to begin a new month, a new season, a new journey in heaven. I felt her today in my yard when I took this photo. I close my eyes and can see her walking on the beach. Her energy is magnificent. Thank you for giving us the strength to get outside and feel the sun today. Thanks to your courage we will all be okay.

We crossed pretty much every item off of the bucket list accept going to Italy. I bet she stops in Florence tonight to see all of the fine art and eat a rum cake. Oh the places she will go. We are honoring mum, grandma, bestie with a single glittering gold starfish on our toe or finger.

June 2 · Lorna Sleeper Brunelle

Ever since I moved into my dorm freshman year at The Boston Conservatory, my mother was the first person I called in the morning and the last person I called before bed. Tonight I find myself sitting alone in my home. I really want to call to tell mum about the starfish I had painted on my finger and toe. I may photograph my finger and toe and text her the pic.

I am trying to maintain a clear, focused and peaceful state so that I may hear, feel, see or smell any sign she sends. Wanda has been running around making memories since July of 2013. Some may say she has been running around stockpiling adventures since her first diagnosis in June of 2009. This many miles of running and this much excitement calls for a rest.

I pray the serenity in this respite without mum physically here by my side enables me to sharpen my ability to look through the thin veil between heaven and earth. I hope to be able to see her beauty and feel her love in everything around me. Why must there be a divide between here and eternal paradise? Why must anyone ever be left behind? Why isn't the phone reception in heaven more state-of-the-art?

I know mum can see my starfish nail art. I'd just love to hear whether or not she would have used OPI Cajun Shrimp and Bubble Bath for the base. Or would she have selected some other favorite color combo to make the starfish look especially epic. Epic. She loved to use the word EPIC.

Mum - if you are reading this, whisper "Epic" in my ear. I am waiting for you to become a spiritual show off. You can do it! Ready, set, GO! If you do, it will be epic.

As the notes about Wanda continued to pile up, I couldn't help but notice the common theme. Almost everyone said she was the mother they always wanted, or the mother they wanted to be around when they were young. Wanda was fun, hip, and adventurous, not to mention a fabulous cook. What was her secret? I think a few clues lie within this note I posted three months before she died.

Lorna Sleeper Brunelle February 6, 2014

On this, my 43rd birthday, I want to thank my mother Wanda Stairs Howard for more than four decades of unconditional love. We live in an age of children owning iPods, iPads, laptops, cell phones, DS games and a whole bunch of electronic madness. The greatest gifts children can receive are time, compassion and love. Wanda showered us with an abundance of all three things.

TIME - Educational day trips, beach excursions, arts and crafts projects, science fair projects & book reports, cooking, reading, coloring, singing and playing together, puzzles, Candy Land, Life, Monopoly, Uno, Crazy 8's, Old Maid, library visits, museums, ferry rides, train rides, bike rides, car rides, strolling through the city - we were always together.

COMPASSION - I will always remember the first time I saw my mother hand a homeless person her money. A former volunteer for Catholic Charities and a former hospice employee, our mother is an angel to the sick, a friend to the downtrodden and a blessing to anyone in need.

LOVE - Mum raised us with enough love to fill oceans and tie ribbons around the globe.

How lucky I was to have shared these 43 birthdays with the woman who began this journey with me on February 6, 1971. Today is your day, too, mum. I love ya more than a thinly pounded breaded chicken cutlet, dusted with high-end Romano and Parmesan cheese, fried in extra virgin olive oil. Thank you for having me.

The recipe to make a legacy of love is time, mixed with compassion, and sprinkled with a whole lot of love. Her legacy of love was the concept for her obituary. Mum prepared every aspect of her burial arrangements but neglected to prepare the obituary.

I found myself sitting at a blank page on my computer screen for over an hour trying to figure out where to begin. We were blessed with a bond that is rarer than most people claim. Our relationship became even stronger during the final year of her life. We were connected spiritually by a sense of *knowing*.

One day I called a Chinese food restaurant near Wanda's house. I ordered her a surprise delivery of chicken chow mein with crunchy noodles, boneless pork strips, and ribs on the bone. Mum awoke from a nap craving the *exact* same meal. Within minutes the food was at her door. We were that connected.

How on earth would I be able to remove myself from this level of understanding to write an appropriate obituary? Would people understand the true measure of her worth in a few paragraphs? Without her around to proofread my copy how would I ever know if she approved of the final draft?

More importantly, how would I capture and convey the truly remarkable essence of Wanda? As a single mother she sang us lullabies and always managed to provide us with an abundance of love, adequate clothing, and an unending supply of art, music, confidence, faith, and hope. She, on a shoestring budget, took us on adventures and day trips. Mum understood the value of creativity and colored on the placemats in restaurants.

Wanda, who kept her own peanut butter jar separate from my stepfather Doug's peanut butter jar because she wanted to live in a world free of butter and jelly smears and toast crumbs. Wanda, who valiantly taught us how to live as she prepared to die...How would I fit her life in her obituary?

I began with bullet points of what seemed to matter the most. Try as I may, I could not land the opening sentence. Remembering mum's passionate discussions about how much she loathed the phrase, "She lost her battle to breast cancer" I leaned on my friend Jennifer (a writer and lifelong family friend) for support with the wording in the opening of the obituary.

Wanda was *not* a loser. She was a champion. The message had to be crystal clear. Mum wanted to message every news anchor in America, begging them to stop saying people "lost their battle with cancer" on air. She was convinced the media could change the way in which we perceive death by cancer.

After a few concentrated hours at the computer and with final approval from mum's husband and my sisters, this is the draft that went to the newspapers.

Wanda M. (Stairs) Howard, 59, a capable and strong warrior, claimed victory over cancer June 1, 2014, her courageous spirit released from its earthly challenges to soar into peace and joy. She battled the disease with a champion's heart, relishing her life for as long as her body would allow. She was at home surrounded by her family. Born July 19, 1954, in Waltham, she was the daughter of the late Raymond L. Stairs and Constance M. (Gandolfo) Williams. Wanda worked behind an artistic eye to bring color and life to the newspaper advertising field for many years, though her favorite career moments were spent working for the Taunton Visiting Nurses Association. Wanda's compassionate heart brought comfort to many cherished hospice patients. Her giving soul motivated her volunteer work with Catholic Charities. She loved art, painting, singing, fashion, gardening, cooking, the ocean, helping those in need and fostering creativity in all around her. But most of all, Wanda's greatest joy was being a mother and grandmother. She devoted her life to building a legacy of love. Survivors include her husband, Douglas Howard of Buzzard's Bay; her daughters, Lorna J. Brunelle and her husband Roger, Elizabeth E. Poirier and her husband Kenneth and Tahlia R. Mann and her husband Lincoln, all of Middleboro; her grandchildren, Paige E. Miranda, Tyler S. Lambert, Taylor L. Poirier and Trey A. Mann; her best friend, Linda Fratus; and her dog Emma Mae. She was predeceased by her brother, Raymond L. Stairs. Calling hours were held from 4-7 p.m. Saturday, June 7, 2014, at the Chapman, Cole & Gleason Funeral Home, located at 2599 Cranberry Highway (Rte. 28), in Wareham. A celebration of life was held at 7 p.m. A private burial will be held at St. Patrick's Cemetery in Watertown.

The next little hiccup occurred when we realized we didn't have a typical "obit" photo. We had spent ten months taking photos of our mother but never considered the obit picture. Nearly every photo we had included our mother with the grandchildren, endless selfies, her dog Emma, a plate of food or the ocean in the background. We never stopped to take a single straight shot of her smiling face.

We ended up selecting a great photo of her that was taken on her deck. We cropped everyone out of the picture which left her with a piece of her stylish hair tucked behind one ear, revealing her fashionable earring. This warm image captured her authentic spirit.

Wanda wanted a relaxed, beach vibe at her wake. We decided to dress her in a thin, turquoise blue summer sweater and black leggings for the viewing. The outfit was accessorized with her favorite gold hoop earrings. Around her neck she would wear her gold chain necklace with her Madonna pendant and cross.

Our family set aside flip flops, long beach skirts, sun dresses, and linen pants for the wake, and each of us would be sporting shades of blue. The floral arrangements were ordered with starfish, shells, and beach themes. Our favorite photos of mum were enlarged to 18" x 24" foam board and were displayed throughout the funeral home. As we sorted through the gorgeous photos of Wanda we decided to ask the funeral home director if I could prepare her hair and makeup. The answer was yes.

I packed mum's makeup bag and hair styling tools, determined to recreate her look. We wanted to be sure people recognized her in the casket. There is nothing worse than hearing people whispering disapproving commentary at wakes and funerals. Sentences such as, "Gosh, you could hardly recognize her at the end" or "She was so beautiful back in the day" had no room at Wanda's services. She would be the belle of the ball.

My sister Elizabeth watched the children at home while my sister Tahlia and my husband Roger accompanied me to the funeral home. The director of the home briefed us on what to expect. Mum had been dressed, but they left her face and hair for us to complete. Before long I was setting up her makeup on a little side table next to her body in the coffin.

She looked absolutely beautiful before I began applying her makeup. Her face looked peaceful and happy. We spoke to her the entire time we dolled her up. "You look so pretty, mum" and "We are so proud of you" were part of every stroke of the blush brush and mascara. "No sky blue 1960's eye shadow here, mum. We brought your colors from home. You are going to look epic."

My husband, our captain, watched over us like a protective gargoyle. "You are doing great," he'd say. "She looks really awesome." In order to perfect the eyebrow pencil over her left eye I had to gently rest my body on her chest. Her warm love radiated through the cold, hard shell that was left behind. I knew she was near to us, pleased with the finished product. There wasn't a single moment that I was freaked out or afraid. All I felt was her love. This was an image I never wanted to forget. I took out my phone and snapped a few photos of her lying peacefully, with perfectly contoured eyebrows in the casket.

Wanda prepared to be pretty at her service during the final week in the hospital bed. Her prednisone puffiness had minimized. Her face was thinner and radiant. She was ready for her final party. As a team, we made sure the tattoo of her ugly starfish peeked out from below the three-quarter sleeve on her summer sweater during the viewing.

The inked image reminding us that it is never too late to change or try something new and that life is perfectly flawed.

Wanda Stairs Howard May 6, 2014 · North Truro, MA ·

When we got home last night the sky was a brilliant
gold on the calmest and glass-like sea.

Since our arrival, the ocean has never been
so still. Mother Nature at her best.

38

People Thrive When They Feel Loved

OUR FAMILY ARRIVED EARLY TO THE funeral home to put the finishing touches on everything. We sprayed mum's favorite perfume (Jimmy Choo) throughout the rooms so it smelled like mum's house. We read the cards on the flowers and set up the photos. We were blown away by how many flowers were in the room. This shouldn't have come as a big surprise. Anyone close to Wanda was privy to a fabulous moment of honesty weeks before she died.

When asked if she wanted to offer an "in lieu of flowers" donation for a cancer charity at the wake she said, "Screw that, I want flowers!" She went on to say, "I want flowers everywhere. I am old school. In my day, people sent flowers. I don't care for this donation stuff. You make donations to your favorite charities at Christmas. I want flowers at my funeral. Flowers. All over the room. Flowers." You can imagine how tempted I was to add the following line to her obituary, "In lieu of donations to cancer charities, Wanda would like flowers all over the funeral home."

On the legacy video Wanda said we could only be sad for one day. She didn't want us crying all over her celebration of life at the funeral home. She wanted us to laugh. She wanted us to remember her. She wanted us to be happy. Out of respect for her, we smiled and greeted hundreds of people (many of whom were sobbing) in the receiving line. I never cried. I smiled and tried to remember happier times. If ever I felt tears creeping into my eyes I would look at the flowers and remember her saying, "Screw that!"

As hordes of people told us how Wanda had changed their feelings about living, death, and dying, I knew she was smiling, too. Her mission was accomplished. She had changed the way people thought about dying. An acquaintance said experiencing the last ten months of Wanda's life through Facebook was one of the most important journeys she had ever taken. She said the way in which our mother lived and died helped her come to terms with the death of her own father. Moments like this made me smile.

Wanda had mapped out the entire service. She even ordered her own flowers from Winston's. There were to be no pink ribbons in sight. After mum's second dance with cancer she encouraged everyone to rethink pink. She was disgusted to learn of the high salaries paid to the CEOs of many high profile breast cancer charities. In some cases, less than 20% of the money raised by donations (from people like Wanda) went to help people with cancer. This broke her heart and infuriated her at the same time.

No stone would remain unturned at mum's celebration of life. She even took the time to write the transitions for people to read as we went through the program. She was her own party planner. This made the experience a lot easier for all of us because we knew exactly what Wanda wanted at her send off.

She concluded the service with the song The Voice Within by Christina Aguilera. The lyrics read, "Young girl, don't cry. I'll be right here when your world starts to fall. Young girl, it's alright. Your tears will dry, you'll soon be free to fly."

As the people began to disperse out of the funeral home we gathered around to take a photo. Team Wanda turned out in force and lined up. I snapped pictures of mum in the casket and the grandchildren near the casket with all of the flowers around them. Years from now I want to be able to remember every minute of her farewell. Later that night, I noticed a blue hue over the photo. This had never happened before with my phone, so I took this as a sign from mum.

Team Wanda divided up the flowers. I decided to plant a memory garden with all of the perennials. We set aside roses for my friend who offered to have jewelry made from the petals. We removed the starfish and shells from the arrangements. We removed the earrings and necklace from her body. The time had come to say goodbye to her physical body.

Wanda decided on cremation. This was going to be the last time we would ever see her. Despite this overwhelming reality, I didn't cry. I took her advice and focused on the good. I envisioned her smiling in heaven with her family. I focused on her journey and everything she had overcome. I remembered our promise not to be sad.

Later that night we gathered at her house. Over clam chowder and sandwiches we shared stories and laughed until we were too tired to laugh anymore. I posted pictures of mum on Facebook and thanked everyone for their support. As I posted the photos, I was astounded by mum's appearance in the pictures taken two weeks prior in Truro. She was swollen and puffy. Her ankles were purple and red and doubled in size. Her body was shutting down. We just didn't see it. We only saw her glorious spirit and her will to fill every moment of her life with joy.

The hospice team never called our attention to the telltale signs that she was slipping away from us. Perhaps they assumed we saw what they saw. Perhaps they have experienced people living far past the puffy ankles and skin. If they had warned us what would it have changed? Mum lived and died on her own terms. She was the star on the stage. We merely cheered her on from the wings and in the audience.

Before Wanda died she took the time to write each of us a note and these letters were kept in her funeral box. That week I read the letter she wrote me. She said she wished she had hugged me more as a child. She said that I was extremely grown up for my age (mentally and physically) and therefore she treated me more like an adult than a little girl. She deeply regretted this.

Lucky for her, I have never been much of a hugger. I never felt a lack of love from her. In the note she made it clear children should be hugged and kissed every day. She wanted children to hear the words, "I love you" or be made to feel special every day. In her memory, I made a conscious decision to try to maintain the foundation that she started building with her grandchildren. This advice was a life lesson. If people feel loved they will thrive.

The following week I prepared for our local Relay for Life event. I have sung at the opening ceremony since I had cancer in 2004. After mum's diagnosis in 2009 my entire family became involved with the event. Mum sponsored Team G.G. in honor of her father who died of lung cancer. I have a vivid memory of our mother dressed in a pink sundress releasing white doves on the field during the 2010 ceremony. A few of the doves didn't feel like flying, so she and my friend Bob gently tapped their bottoms to get them going.

Mum, my sisters and the grandchildren slept in a tent on the Relay for Life field that year. It rained all night. Luckily, Wanda loved the rain. On Facebook she frequently posted a picture of the definition of the word pluviophile - a lover of the rain; someone who finds joy and peace of mind during rainy days.

Despite the soggy surroundings, Wanda wanted to be a part of the Relay for Life luminaria event. She loved sharing this experience with her family.

Little did we know the Relay committee had decided to honor Wanda (the week after she died) during the 2014 event. After I sang at the opening ceremony the Mistress of Ceremonies said a few words about mum and asked for a moment of silence in observance of Wanda and the way in which she lived her life. I remember looking at my sister across the grass. We were both holding back tears.

Afterwards, we walked over to the team tent of my friends Lisa and Kim. Lisa had been instrumental in collecting buoys for mum's fence. They had an entire booth set up for Wanda. A banner read "#TeamWanda - the Buoy Project" and they had a beach chair set up with a framed photo of her in the chair. A tarpaulin in front of the chair was sand, beach toys, and shells. There was also a table covered with a starfish and seashell tablecloth that had photos of Wanda all over it.

Visibly moved by the beauty of the moment, my sister and I took a photo in front of the display. It was the first time I had cried in public since her death. From there, I was asked to be a banner holder at the front of the Survivors Walk. During our lap around the track I waved to all of the people who loved our mother. Everyone at the "#TeamWanda - the Buoy Project" booth clapped as we walked by. Their hearts were with us as our hearts began to heal.

Many cancer survivors at Relay commented on the online posts and how beautiful it was to share the final months of Wanda's life through Facebook. As the rain dumped down on us we continued to make our way around the track. Wanda loved the rain. She would have loved her buoy project booth. We were surrounded by the power of Wanda's legacy of love.

<u>Wanda Stairs Howard</u> <u>March 30, 2014</u>
Dear Lord, Teach me to trust in you so that the when
the unexpected storms of life come, I will expect peace
in my midst of those storms, knowing that you are near,
you hear my cries, and you are with me and for me.
(Mark 4:37-40)

39

Purge the Clutter

$\mathcal{S}$HORTLY AFTER MUM RETURNED TO HEAVEN, I went to see a production of The Little Prince at my theatre. Based on the Antoine de Saint-Exupéry novella, the play tells the story of a pilot stranded in the desert who meets a young prince who has fallen to Earth from a tiny asteroid. The Little Prince is the third most-translated book in the world.

The Little Prince was not part of our season line-up. It was an add-on show very late in the season. When I put it into the schedule, I had no idea Wanda wouldn't be alive to see the play. The show's opening night was highlighted on her wall calendar. She couldn't wait to see her friend and artist Roger Clark in the role of the King.

As I sat in the theatre with my nephew Trey, I heard the words of Wanda coming through the lines of The Little Prince. It was as if mum was speaking through the young man playing the role. In this moment, Wanda comforted us through art.

Little Prince: I am going back home today.

Aviator: You can't mean this. Tell me this is a bad dream.

Little Prince: The thing that is most important is the thing that is invisible. Like a flower on a star. Just because I am gone, doesn't mean I've gone away.

Aviator: What?

Little Prince: Do you see my star up there?

Aviator: Which one? There are so many.

Little Prince: Maybe that's just as well. Then all the stars will be your friends.

Aviator: What do you mean?

Little Prince: Each night, watch the sun set and see the stars come out. And know that I am there on one of them - living...and laughing. Then all the stars will laugh for you. Please do not come tonight. It will look a little as if I were dying. That is not true. It's just that this body is too heavy for me to carry all the way. Don't be sad. What will be left will be nothing but an old empty shell. There's nothing sad about empty shells, is there?"

In the final moment of the show the Little Prince says, "Let me go on by myself. There now...I am ready." After days of wishing mum had stayed with us a little while longer, I took comfort in the lines of the play. She was ready to begin the next phase of her journey.

The next week Team Wanda followed the instructions in mum's funeral box by relocating 90% of her beach decor to my kitchen. In two days we stripped my kitchen of purple and green cabbage rose-covered curtains and Victorian tea room trinkets. Team Wanda covered a table on my lawn with a FREE sign eight times. Wanda always loved a good spring clean and purge. She hated clutter. She said you could look years younger with a good haircut and pounds lighter with a good clutter purge. It felt fabulous to give away the treasures of many years in order to provide space for mum's beach theme.

My kitchen got a fresh coat of beach grass green paint and mum's beach art was hung all over the walls. The mantle above the stove was adorned with Japanese glass buoys and the windows were lined with starfish. The window treatments were replaced with a simple single strand rope garland with shells and starfish. This allowed even more light to flood into the kitchen each morning. We added rose geranium plants, sea grass, and an orchid to bring oxygen to the space.

At the end of the weekend we were able to sit in "mum's" kitchen in my home. One may think it odd to leave my stepfather Doug with blank kitchen walls in his house so soon after mum's death, but since this was mum's wish he was the first to ask when we would be packing up her things.

Once the kitchen project was complete my husband Roger took me to Cape Cod for the weekend. We stayed in Dennisport. The hotel was next door to a place my family stayed for over ten years before it was converted to condos. I was extremely sad when I packed for our getaway. Everything in my travel bag told the story of travels with mum. A toothbrush from the store in Truro. Hand cream from the spa at Wentworth. Chocolates from the turn down service at bedtime.

I began to cry as we pulled into the hotel. I couldn't help but remember happier and healthier times with our beautiful mother on Cape Cod. As Roger and I headed to the front of the hotel the first car I saw in the parking lot had a bumper sticker that read "Watertown Is My Hometown." Watertown was Wanda's hometown. I considered this a sign from mum in heaven reminding me that she was with me at the beach. I photographed the bumper sticker and posted it on Facebook. The response from the post was awesome. Team Wanda was impressed with her early ability to send signs.

To date, I have had one dream about Wanda. In my dream Linda and I were walking in Cambridge. We had just had breakfast in mum's favorite deli, which is known for its potato pancakes. As we stopped at the curb to cross the street I turned around and saw mum. She was very thin and appeared to be in her mid-twenties. Her hair was in a perfect ponytail and her bangs blew in the breeze. She was extremely tan. Her tanned skin was a beautiful contrast to a hot pink nightgown. When I spotted her I yelled, "Linda! She is here. Mum is here. She is walking toward us." Just then mum looked at me with sparkly eyes. In a very excited voice (as if to say, can you believe I can already do this) she said, "HI!" And just like that, I woke up.

A week after our brief stay in Dennisport we buried Wanda's ashes at the cemetery. The weeks between the wake and the burial allowed us to catch our breath and adjust to our new normal. For Team Wanda, the new normal involved being together every single day. Each morning began with a group text between all of us. The first person would write, "What are we up to today?" One of us would write back with an idea or a plan.

I would often write back "I have a pitcher of iced coffee and lunch meat? Sandwiches? Manicures? Beach?" We would sit together for hours going over and over every detail of the past year. Sometimes crying, always laughing, and desperately trying to stay busy. We had run around for ten straight months and no one was ready to slow down. To slow down would be to grieve. Mum hadn't allowed us to be sad.

The day before the burial we set up tables and chairs for the reception after the burial. Together we spray-painted gold glitter and ocean blue starfish, which were displayed on each table. The centerpieces were mason jars filled with roses and sprays of sea grass. My friend Kim decorated the cake for us. The words Team Wanda were displayed in blue with a border of edible candy seashells and starfish.

We set up a memory table. The Buoy Project Team Wanda banner from Relay for Life covered the table. On top of it sat a few of the things Wanda loved. Pictures of the family, a gargoyle, her favorite photo of herself, a picture of the cottages in Truro, her favorite hand cream, her favorite vase, shells, the image of Madonna Lady of the Streets, and bouquets of roses, hydrangea, and sea grass.

We had an Adirondack chair filled with buoys next to the table. Buoys were visible all around the yard. Family friends Theresa and Kim prepared foods that she loved. They had the meal ready for us to serve under a tent upon our return from the burial.

July 11, 2014 (the day of the burial) was beautiful. There wasn't a cloud in the early July sky. We lined up the caravan of vehicles at my house. Dressed in casual summer clothes we posed for photos in the yard. The trunk of my Jeep was packed with the enlarged photos we displayed at the wake, starfish, her cremation remains, and dozens of multicolored long-stemmed roses.

Days prior, my husband Roger filled little glass bottles with mum's ashes. Members of Team Wanda were invited to take a cork top bottle of ashes (which appeared to be filled with beach sand) as they parted from the burial reception. We were also sure to save a small portion of her remains for anyone who was unable to attend the service.

We set up a small table at the grave with her starfish blanket, a few framed photos, and the box of mum's remains. We rested the oversized photos of her along the grave and placed starfish everywhere. After a brief graveside service, I sang Amazing Grace and we all placed our flowers on mum's grave. The box of her remains was placed in a hole near her grave. My nephew Tyler (mum's first grandson) began placing roses on top of the box in the hole, then all of the other grandchildren followed this.

Next, something really cool happened. The grandchildren took turns using a shovel to gently place dirt on top of the box. Each of the four grandchildren helped to bury their grandmother, our mother. This was one of the most beautiful memories I have of the day. I was so moved I photographed each of them burying her.

Looking back, I don't remember where the shovel came from. I assume it was near the grave for the cemetery staff to use once we had cleared out. No one ever prompted them to shovel dirt over the remains, it was an instinct to take care of gram. To cover her. To protect her. To lay her to rest.

Once the grave was filled with dirt we held a photo of mum and stood behind and around the sides of her grave. Holding up the photos, we posed for a full circle Team Wanda photo. Mum's headstone (with the newly added Lily of the Valley flowers and date of her death) was proudly centered in the photo. Her grave site was surrounded by her team holding images of her beautiful smile.

The purity of her legacy of love was preserved in a picture. She had worked tirelessly throughout her entire life to become the love nucleus of the family. She had succeeded. It was time for her to rest. It was time for us to carry on where she left off.

Elizabeth was one of the few who left her cell phone in the car during the service and as we were walking away she decided to get her phone to take a photo of mum's decorated grave. After a quiet moment alone at the site she spoke to mum and leaned down to kiss her grave. At this exact moment her phone rang and the song "Happy" played. A kiss from heaven.

The following weekend, on July 19th, we celebrated our mother's 60th birthday. In true Team Wanda fashion, we had a beautiful backyard brunch with all of her favorite people, puppies and food. We drove to the Armenian market in Watertown and picked up olives, cheese, and her absolute favorite flat bread Armenian pizza, Lamejun.

Linda's newest puppy Rosie (who was named by our mother before she died) made her debut. Part Boston terrier and part pug, her breed is known as a "bug". Rosie filled our minds with joy rather than pain on our milestone morning. When prone to tears we took turns holding Emma Mae and Rosie.

I woke up feeling a little lost on mum's birthday. I spent some time going through the pages of a beautiful Facebook scrapbook our friend Gina gifted us. By using a program called My Social Book, Gina collected all of the Facebook posts and photos from mum's final week on earth. She placed them in three bound books, one for each of Wanda's daughters. I recommend this gift (mysocialbook.com) for anyone who has experienced a life changing event.

After rereading all of the messages that were posted to our mother's Facebook page I meditated. The scrapbook and the meditation brought me to the thoughts in this note.

Lorna Sleeper Brunelle post to Wanda Stairs Howard July 19, 2014 ·

Today is my mother's 60th birthday. My mother was born on her father Raymond's birthday. Every July 19th we had two candles on the cake, one for Grandpa Ray and one for mum. We will blow out two candles on a cake today even though both of them have returned to heaven.

I posted a lot about mum during her final days on earth this year between May 27 and June 1, 2014. Those who know us really well remember that a year ago today, we celebrated mom's 59th birthday on the 11th floor of the Bigelow building of The Massachusetts General Hospital. Nine days prior, an ER team of doctors admitted mum after having shoved a huge tube through the side of her body into her lung (without pain meds) to drain 3.5 liters of fluid.

As mum fought for her life on ten liters of oxygen, Team Wanda sat vigil around her hospital bed round the clock waiting to hear what caused the fluid to build up in her lung. During those long and stressful days, we realized the importance of time. We all prayed God would grant us more minutes, more hours, more days with mum.

Day nine of her hospital stay (mum's 59th birthday) is the day she learned that the breast cancer she had beat in 2009 had returned and metastasized to her lung and liver. Days later we realized the cancer had also spread to her bones. Ten months of non-stop bucket-listing began the moment mum was discharged from the hospital. The optimist in me never believed my mother would spend her last earthly birthday in the hospital.

Today, I cannot help but remember how mum spent her second to last birthday on earth. A year prior to the Mass Gen birthday, our family randomly decided to celebrate mum's 58th birthday at the Brazilian Grille in Hyannis. The day fell on a Thursday. Everyone had busy schedules. We had to work the next day.

Despite all of this, we all ended up around a table to celebrate mum. After dinner, we walked up and down Main Street poking into the shops. The grandchildren loved their time in the joke shop with mum. The perfect night ended with the kids riding on the old fashioned carousel and us posing for a family photo near a ridiculously oversized Adirondack chair.

On the way home mum said it was one of the best birthdays of her life. We didn't have a crystal ball to reveal that mum's next birthday would entail a hospital room, tubes, oxygen, IV lines and the diagnosis of a terminal illness. None of us knew mum's Hyannis birthday in the summer of 2012 would be her last birthday filled with good health and hope for more birthdays.

I am so damn grateful that we dropped everything to celebrate mum's 58th birthday on the Cape. It wasn't a "Big Birthday." She wasn't turning 21, or 30 or 40 or 50 or 60 but we celebrated big and created a big memory.

If I learned anything during the last ten months of mum's life, I learned that we must always live in the moment. We have to honor and celebrate the people we love every day. We have to treat every birthday as if it is a "big" birthday. Every moment as if it is a big moment. Life is a gift. A privilege. Who are we to downplay or downsize the beauty of every day here on earth? The photos I have selected for this post tell the story. In an instant everything can change.

July 19, 2012 - one of the best times in mum's life

July 19, 2013 - one of the scariest times in mum's life.

July 19, 2014 - one of the saddest times in our lives as we celebrate mum's birthday without her.

As my family blows out the candles for mum and Grandpa Ray today, I am going to make a wish. My wish is for everyone to treat the little moments in their lives as if they are giant life moments. If we had waited to celebrate mum's "big 60th" birthday today, we wouldn't have had the chance to be with her.

During the final ten months of mum's life she'd begin most mornings by stating a mantra of gratitude. When I close my eyes, I can hear clapping and saying, "Today is going to be awesome! (insert rapid clapping) I can't wait. Every day I have something fun to look forward to. Today we are going to make more memories. We have another day. How lucky are we?!"

How lucky we were to have that extra time. Time is the one thing we should never take for granted. On mum's "Big 60th birthday" I encourage you to make the pockets in your busy schedules for happiness, and enjoy every second with those you love. Rinse and Repeat.

Don't save the celebrations for the big moments
because in the big picture, all of the moments are
big. (insert rapid clapping) Love, Lorna

The day after the birthday brunch, Team Wanda went to mum's favorite zoo. This was one of her many happy places. Eager to keep a piece of her on earth with us, we longed to conjure the memories of her talking to Joey (the highly inappropriate monkey) and excitedly grabbing the grandkids on the train ride to call attention to an elk she spotted in the distance. If ever we were to feel Wanda with us, it would be at the zoo or the beach.

This weekend was also the closing performance of Peter Pan at my theatre. Wanda named the place The Alley Theatre because a century ago it was a bowling alley. The director (my friend Melissa) took our breath away with a stunning preshow tribute to Wanda, my stepson Brent, and Dorothy the sister of our choreographer Lucy. All three lives were directly connected to theatre and all three returned to heaven in 2014.

Three huge photos of the three lost loved ones covered the back wall of the theatre. In the middle, the following perfect line from Peter Pan was projected. "You know that place between sleep and awake, the place where you still remember dreaming? That's where I will always love you. That's where I will be waiting." - Peter Pan

Wanda Stairs Howard May 25, 2014 · Buzzards Bay, MA ·

Sand...some of the best stuff ever!

40

Children Can Handle the Truth

URING THE WEEKS THAT FOLLOWED WANDA'S transition, we talked about her every day. We found comfort by welcoming her into the conversation through a memory or story. My husband said the thing that set her apart from other parents was her willingness to have our backs. He said he had never seen a parent defend or support her children the way Wanda had supported us our entire lives.

My sisters and I shared stories about the times Wanda went nuts on a person who had mistreated us. Her mama lion loyalty was fierce. When the injustice involved children being mean to her children, she had her own special way of dealing with the playground, school hall, or bus bully. She skipped right over writing a note to the bus driver or classroom teacher. She would call the principal, request a meeting, and see to it that all eyes were watching until order was restored. Yes, she was *that* mother. If the situation persisted she found a way to reach out to the parents of the child.

If the situation involved an adult mistreating her children the game dramatically changed. I got my period when I was nine years old. I will never forget the day my teacher (who had never been warm and fuzzy with me) gave me a hard time about using the restroom. "You were in the bathroom fifteen minutes ago, Lorna" she said. "Hold it. You can wait."

After a few minutes I raised my hand and asked to go to the nurse. "Fine!" the teacher barked back at me. I was afraid the nurse would make me stay at school with a visible stain on my pants. En route to the nurse's office I stopped at the pay phone in the lobby and called my mother. As soon as I heard her voice I began to cry. Once she listened to my account of what happened she said, "Tell me the truth, Lorna. Were you disrespectful to your teacher? Did you answer her back? Were you fresh to her?" My answer to all of her questions was "No."

As mum consoled me I heard the voice of my teacher. "Who do you think you are little girl? No one gave you permission to use the phone. You are in big trouble!" (She was using a quietly creepy and threatening voice.) As soon as my mother heard her reprimanding me she said, "I am on my way. Go to the office and wait for me."

Rather than go to the office the teacher made me walk back to the classroom. She scolded me the entire length of the hallway. The notion of having my peers notice the stain on my pants was so mortifying I felt dizzy as I reentered the room.

Before long, I could hear Wanda hollering in the office. "How dare she? How dare any teacher treat any child this way?" Here is how the story ends. I was dismissed from school, mum taught me how to count the cycle and days of my period on the wall calendar in our kitchen, and I was given a Bermuda bag clutch pocketbook to hold my huge adult-sized maxi pads. "You are going to have to be responsible for this, Lorna. I will help you remember your cycle, but we have to be a team on this and work together. Life is messy sometimes. When we have bad days we have to learn from them and become stronger."

The next day we had a meeting and the teacher apologized in front of her boss, Wanda, and me. For the rest of the year my teacher remained annoyed by my presence in her class.

When I think about this story I am struck by the memory of mum taking the time to ask if I had been disrespectful to the teacher. Mum's limitless love was unconditional, but honesty was revered in her house. Honesty was at the front of her parenting toolbox. "I never lie to my children," she would say with great pride. "It's all in presentation. You can tell people the truth without hurting them if you do it the right way."

Honesty and truth filled every sentence when Wanda told her grandchildren she was going to die. She said, "I will love you and stay with you as long as I possibly can, and we will have an epic time, but eventually, I am going to die." My sister Liz loves to tell the stories about how mum used humor when handling this topic. One day Wanda was talking to the two youngest grandchildren about the preparation for her journey back to heaven. During the talk, my nephew Trey placed his head down on the table.

In a concerned voice, Wanda looked at Trey and said, "What's the matter? Are you upset because I am going to die?" After a pause Trey lifted his head and said, "No." With a look of shock on her face Wanda said, "Well, you should be." Meaning, it is okay to be just a wee bit sad for a quick second or so. Grandma Wanda was, after all, pretty awesome. The kids started laughing as soon as Wanda blurted out the tongue in cheek comeback.

Wanda also promised never to shut the children out. She vowed to involve them in every step of the way. "We all die," she would say. "There isn't anything scary or awful about it. I think the idea of going to heaven is beautiful. I will still get to check in on all of you from time to time. I am never leaving you for good."

We honored mum's core values of honesty and truth during her entire journey back home. Where many families decide to keep the children on the other side of the hospice deathbed door, we gave the grandkids a seat front and center. We encouraged them to read to mum, massage her hands, comb her hair, and talk to her. We answered all of their questions and maintained an ongoing dialogue about mum's transition to heaven.

Seeing the children love and care for mum during these precious days was, in many ways, the most powerful part of the experience. Their affectionate doting on their grandmother was part of their healing process. I am convinced their invitation to actively love their grandmother right up until her last breath is why Wanda's final days were filled with so much peace. Honesty and love paved Wanda's path back to heaven.

<u>Wanda Stairs Howard March 29, 2014</u>

Fun day to look forward to! The two youngest grand babies are on their way so we can bake peanut butter cookies, pistachio pudding and chocolate cupcakes with homemade frosting. I'm excited to make more memories. Since standing too long is hard for me they're going to love being responsible and doing it all themselves with just a little supervision from Gram.

41

Hospitality and Hugs Matter

RIENDS I HAVE KNOWN SINCE GRAMMAR school visited me that summer bringing bags filled with gourmet food. As we feasted on truffle mushroom, and pasta with parm cheese, my friend Heather shared a story she had never mentioned in the thirty-plus years of our friendship. She recalled the day her father died of a heart attack in their home when she was a little girl. She remembered feeling him physically hug her moments after he died. She recounted the story with certainty and grace.

As she spoke my mind drifted back to the moment right after mum died. I remained at the foot of her bed sobbing with my head resting near her feet. At one point I felt someone embrace the back of my body. My entire body became warm. For a second I thought my husband had leaned on me to offer comfort, but within seconds I realized no one was in the room with me. I had forgotten this moment until my friend recounted the story about her father's heavenly hug.

When my friends left that night my husband shared a similar story. He, too, felt a hug from heaven after his son died. He, too, was in a deep state of grief when he felt the embrace from beyond. To date, everyone I have shared these stories with has experienced a similar hug from heaven.

Wanda often spoke of the thin veil between the living and the afterlife. She promised she would demonstrate her ability to continue loving us from a higher spirit level after her death. The distance between heaven and earth seems much closer when sharing these stories.

Trey was the first of the four grandchildren to have a birthday after mum went to heaven. He was turning double digits and when asked what he wanted for his birthday meal, the soon to be ten-year-old said, "meatloaf." We planned a dinner party at my house for a huge Team Wanda dinner. In Wanda fashion, we had enough food to feed all of heaven. We honored mum's legacy of love through family traditions.

Keeping up with tradition, we went to Doug's house for dinner the following week. This was a little weird for all of us because we hadn't visited their house a lot since mum died. We could tell she was pleased to see all of us around her table once again. The evidence was in a sign she sent.

The country was having a good time purchasing Coca-Cola bottles with random names (Have a Coke with MELISSA, DAVID, MIKE, or SARAH) printed on the label. People were flocking to the stores in search of their name on a bottle. Doug, who was oblivious to this trend, filled his fridge with a bottle of Coke, another bottle of soda, juice, and bottled water for our dinner. Imagine our surprise when we sat at the table with a bottle of Coke that had the word TEAM written on it. My niece Taylor took a Sharpie and wrote WANDA under the word TEAM on the Coke bottle.

We kept up the weekly dinners together and instituted Sunday brunch at my place. We never skipped a Sunday. Everyone on Team Wanda knew I would always be serving food around 9:30 a.m. on Sunday morning. This was a way for us to check in and support each other during our healing and readjustment process.

It was around this time I received an elated call from my sister Tahlia. She was speaking so quickly and loudly I had a hard time deciphering her words as she said, "I just woke up. I finally had a dream about her! She finally came to me in a dream." This was the happiest I had heard my sister since the final week of our mother's life. She went on to say, "Mum was sitting up on her bed. She knew she had died. She knew she only had a short amount of time to talk to me. It was real. I *legit* was just talking to mum. I didn't want it to end. She looked awesome and we had the best talk. Finally. She finally came to me."

There are restorative benefits to dreaming this vividly. In this brief moment the people on earth are granted visitation with their most precious souls in heaven. This ethereal time together seeing, hearing, holding, smelling, and feeling your loved one is priceless. These types of dreams or heavenly visits started when I began to quiet my mind: turning off the TV, silencing the cell phone, and meditating every morning and most nights was paramount to my healing.

Before we knew it summer had slipped away. The youngest two of the four grandchildren were picking out back-to-school clothes and yellow buses were back on the streets. This was the first time grandma Wanda wouldn't be at the bus stop for the first day of school. It was the first time she wouldn't be calling the kids to ask about their new classroom and teacher.

The start of the new season stung more than I expected. The idea of autumn changing the color of the leaves without our mother seemed strangely cruel. I cried alone in the shower minutes after my friend called to say that my annual bushel of Honey Crisp apples was ready for pick up. This would be the first year I wouldn't make mum endless amounts of apple pie, cream cheese dip, and apple crisp.

In mum's honor, we decided to have a series of late summer/early fall fundraisers for the St. Jude Children's Research Hospital. This was one of Wanda's favorite charity organizations. We planned one of the trendy paint nights where guests paint on canvas while sipping wine. The other event was a comedy show.

These festivities were a great distraction from the weeks without mum. The good cause and common goal gave us something positive to focus on. Family togetherness meant everything to Wanda. She wanted to be sure we saw each other weekly after she left. These events were another way of keeping the extended team together.

Team Wanda had strong representation at the paint night. The theme was End of Summer. The scene was a starfish in the sand on a beach. Out of the forty-plus people who painted, thirty of them were members of Team Wanda. We collected fabulous raffle items. The most sought after item was a beautiful Coach pocketbook donated by my friend Carol. My sister Tahlia coveted the bag the days leading up to the event.

The paint night was the same weekend as Tahlia's birthday. Tal was the first of us sisters to celebrate a birthday without mum. Tahlia's son Trey shook the bag of raffle tickets profusely on stage in front of the painting patrons and my friend Maureen pulled the winning name. My sister Tahlia (who doesn't often win anything) won the bag.

In our eyes mum was sending Tal a birthday gift from heaven. Each time a birthday for someone on Team Wanda arrived, I went through mum's Facebook page and shared the post she sent them the year prior when she was alive. She always made time to write heartfelt birthday notes. Making people feel special was her art form.

Everyone felt welcome in the company of our mother. There was always a plate of food or cup of coffee in her hands. Her ability to nurture people was one of her most beautiful attributes. It is imperative that we keep this part of her essence alive.

As colder winds blew into New England, I made my way through each new day mirroring her example. Her influence of love, food, and family was visible in every pretty table we set for every hearty meal we served. I am so grateful to have inherited this ability. I am not a coffee drinker, but since her return to heaven I have become the family barista. I have made *a lot* of coffee.

My kitchen is the new meeting spot. We have gotten together almost every day since mum's absence. When I see my nieces and nephews at my table I am reminded of the decades of time chronicled through pictures of mum sitting with us at her table. As I plate pastina, chicken and basil for the kids, I remember Wanda doting on us. In these moments I thank God we are all together. I whisper a prayer letting mum know I will try to pick up where she left off.

Mum entertained around the table right up until her death. Two weeks before mum returned to heaven she set a perfect table of treats for us at the cottage in Truro. The starfish tablecloth was covered with little vintage bowls of candy, fresh flowers, cheese, fruit, and crackers. The day before she became sedated she plated pastries and served coffee to her guests. Every time I set a pretty table, prepare a perfect cup of coffee, or make someone happy with a great meal I will think of mum.

The following week my sister Liz and I met to discuss the baby shower for my niece. Our mother's first grandchild Paige had just announced that she was going to give birth to our mother's great-grandson, Mason.

It was clear Wanda wanted to be part of the baby shower planning. While I typed notes on my computer screen a beautiful starfish image flashed on my computer. Even more impressive, the photo of the starfish (which rested in the sand in a stunning ocean) became my screensaver. I never touched a button to make this happen. To be honest, I don't know how to make a picture my desktop photo.

I think mum was reminding us that life goes on. We were planning for the birth of a new member of our family while mourning the loss of our matriarch. The circle of life was before our very eyes. It was a time to welcome baby Mason. Mum wasn't going to miss a single second. The thin veil provided her with a perfect view.

<u>Wanda Stairs Howard September 25, 2013</u>

Back in 1979 in about 6 hours a baby girl was born at Tobey Hospital in Wareham. She weighed 6 lbs 5 oz. And had the biggest brown eyes I'd ever seen. If you see her today tell her Happy Birthday. Her name is Tahlia Rae.

42

Everyone Needs a Great Pen

GRANDMOTHER. GRANDFATHER. MOTHER. FATHER. DAUGHTER. SON. Spouse. Uncle. Aunt. Niece. Nephew. Cousin. Friend. Caregiver. Patient. Advocate. Health Care Proxy. The funny one. The reliable one. The creative one. The clever one. The emotional one. The strong one. The understanding one. The organized one. The smart one. The defiant one. The helpful one. The kind one. The stable one. The troubled one. The selfish one. The selfless one. The rebel one. The tragic one. The generous one. The positive one. The negative one. The responsible one. The unhappy one. The educated one. The bitter one. The grateful one. The lost one. The grounded one. We all play a role in our family.

In a flash the dynamic of these relationships can change. What happens next (after the change) is different for everyone. Team Wanda opted to stick together like glue. We stuck pieces of our broken hearts together and created a tapestry. For safe keeping we wrapped the memory of Wanda in this tapestry. Now the tapestry blankets us. When the universe makes a tremendous shift we need to wrap ourselves in love.

For me, the hardest part about life immediately after loss is going through each day without my best friend physically at my side. I picked up the phone to call mum almost every day for the first few months. Some days, I sent a text message to her phone. Silly, I know.

Had the most remarkable day. Wish you were here. Love you.

Had the best time in the North End tonight. You would have loved the meatballs. Miss you.

Paige is starting to show. Baby Mason will be here before we know it. Love you.

Heard a song and thought of you. Miss your voice. Love you.

You will never guess who I met today. Wait...you already know. Cool, huh? Hope heaven is beautiful.

On the hardest days, I picked up a pen and paper and wrote notes to her. As a child, Wanda played school in a makeshift classroom in the cellar of her home in Watertown, Massachusetts. As an adult, she loved new office supplies and swore by the necessity of a great pen. For Wanda the perfect pen needed to be lightweight and easy to grip, with a quick drying, fast flow of ink. She was a staunch believer in the power of handwritten note. I have spent many hours rereading her letters to me.

Wanda had beautiful penmanship. Before bed, we would play Connect the Dots and Hangman at the kitchen table. Wanda would doodle on the margins of paper used for each game. She would write our full names *Wanda Maria, Lorna Jayne, Elizabeth Eve,* and *Tahlia Rae* in pretty cursive along the border of each sheet.

Every time I hold a high quality pen I am reminded of her writing our names on paper. People who knew Wanda often mistake my penmanship for hers. I love it when this happens. When I wasn't writing to mum in pen or via a text message, I was writing about her on Facebook. I posted this note four months after her shift back to heaven.

Lorna Sleeper Brunelle
October 25, 2014

I stopped by mum's grave today after work. I thought for sure all of the rain and wind we had last week would have blown the starfish off of her headstone. As soon as I saw the starfish, I envisioned her saying, "Stop worrying. Everything is okay."

From there, I sat alone at one of our favorite pizza shops and had a slice. After I drove by some of our spots. I ended the day by stopping in mum's favorite bakery in Newton. In her honor, I bought a lobster tail and slice of rum cake.

As different as it was to be in all of these places without her, I took comfort remembering the time we spent in each place. I know so many people who are grieving. In time the seemingly impossible things, such as revisiting a place you once loved without the company of your loved one, may eventually bring you peace.

Today I felt hopeful. In time I may be able to revisit Wentworth, Portsmouth, Beacon Hill, Newbury Street, Truro and all of our other hideaways without the pain of her absence being greater than the happiness I felt with her by my side.

Everything is going to be okay.

With the arrival of the month of November came a mix of emotions. Team Wanda started the month by hosting a baby shower for my niece, Paige. Completely unplanned, we all seemed to be wearing starfish or something that once belonged to Wanda. I welcomed the guests with a few words about family. Midway through I began to cry. As soon as I felt the tears I wrapped up the sentiment.

My unexpected public display of emotion lead to my niece crying. I was so disappointed in myself for upsetting her. As I berated myself my friend Mo said, "You are allowed to show people that you are hurting. Today is a big day. We all feel Wanda's absence. You weren't sobbing up there, you had tears in your eyes. It was lovely that you referred to your mother's legacy of family and love." Hearing this helped turn things around in my brain. Wanda couldn't stomach fake people. To pretend we didn't miss her on days such as this would have been inauthentic.

A few weeks later, we had another first birthday without mum. My niece Taylor turned thirteen. Team Wanda shared cake, ice cream, and laughter. This day there weren't any public tears. My sister Liz hosted Thanksgiving the following week. The meal was perfect. We laughed and shared happy memories. We never gave in to our grief. Wanda would have approved. Thanksgiving was never mum's favorite holiday. Perhaps this is why the first one without her was more tolerable than expected.

Thanksgiving weekend I hosted our annual Artisans of New England event at the theatre. Wanda loved this event. I have the most fabulous pictures of mum at the faire every year. My favorite picture is of her standing beside a vintage, robin egg blue VW bus outside of the theatre. She is wearing an apron from Gloucester covered in pictures of lobsters and shells. She is smiling from ear to ear.

Mum was surrounded by everything she loved at our annual faire. Family, food, creative people, and art. One of her favorite vendors is our friend Donna. She is known as the beef jerky lady. Mum would walk through the faire holding a huge bag of the high end jerky while stopping at each booth to admire the art. She would slip the grandkids money to purchase massive amounts of beef jerky. Happy images of mum at this event are preserved in my memory like a scrapbook.

A year later, tears were parked at the corner of my eyes all day as vendors, artists, and patrons asked about her. I typically only interact with the artists once a year for the faire. Many of the artists had no idea Wanda died. The event (that had once brought all of us tremendous joy) felt like a punishment that first year without mum. Grief grabs us when we least expect it. One would think Thanksgiving would have been harder than an art faire, harder than a baby shower. We simply never know when the sadness will surface and boil over.

I remember walking into the bathroom of the theatre and sitting in a stall for a long while. I asked mum for help getting through the day. I asked her to forgive me for being human and missing her. Moments after, an artist I have known for many years walked over and said, "I just saw your mother walk by my booth and then walk down the hall. She is here. You didn't think she'd miss the faire, did you?"

Another sign. *I hear you mum.*

My ten-year thyroid cancer anniversary was on December 15, 2014. This was the first time mum and I didn't celebrate by heading to the Wentworth by the Sea for spa treatments. More importantly, this was the first time I didn't receive a beautiful, handwritten card reminding me of how far I had come in my recovery. Mum and I were sisters in cancer. I felt her absence more often than not that day. While I was grateful to be a ten-year cancer survivor, I woke up feeling robbed of more time with my mother.

As a thyroid cancer survivor, I have two ultrasounds a year on my neck and a lot of blood work as part of my follow-up care. The first five years of my recovery, I had annual full body scans. Thyroid cancers tend to be very slow growing and compared to breast cancers, they're less likely to recur or spread. I find myself questioning why Wanda's follow-up care for breast cancer merely consist of nothing more than an annual mammogram. Was this the reason her breast cancer had a chance to metastasize to the point that her options were so limited five years after her initial diagnosis?

I'm no medical professional, but I believe the standard course of follow-up care for people with advanced breast cancer should involve an annual MRI which involves less exposure to radiation than bone scans and CT scans. In Wanda's case, five years of clean mammograms didn't serve as preventative medicine or spot the first signs of the cancer's return. I will always wonder what would have happened if Wanda had demanded a more accurate method of follow-up care.

Since my diagnosis, I have written a letter about my recovery on the morning of my cancerversary. This is what I posted on Facebook that year:

Lorna Sleeper- Brunelle <u>December 15, 2014</u>

Ten years ago today I was diagnosed with thyroid cancer. I received the call from my doctor while standing in the driveway of our mother Wanda Stairs Howard's house. For the past nine years, each December 15, mum and I packed a bag and headed to the Wentworth by the Sea for a spa stay.

This morning I woke up reminiscing about the past decade. During a meditation I asked myself what I want for the next ten years. The answer - adventure and time with the people I love. After mum died this June, I asked her husband if I could have her calendar. Her priorities are evident. Adventure and time with the people she loved.

People keep telling me 2015 will be a better year. Truth is, there were some absolutely gorgeous moments in 2014. Right down to mum's beautiful transition to heaven, I am grateful for the time we had in 2014 and for all of the lessons I learned about unconditional love.

> Adventure and time with the people we love...the investment is
> pretty affordable but the value is worth its weight in gold. ♡

The day before Christmas I saw four cars in a row in a parking lot. Each car had a starfish hanging from the rearview mirror. This was mum working her magic. *Okay, now you are just showing off.*

Christmas was mum's favorite holiday. She shopped and cooked for days preparing to host Christmas Eve dinner. That first year without her we decided to order a complete dinner from a local Italian restaurant. We know the owners and appreciated their willingness to lighten our emotional load. The trays of chicken cutlets, ziti, meatballs, and sausage eliminated the stress of preparing this iconic meal without mum. This was a much-needed break, as our ability to rise above our grief during the holiday season was minimizing.

After the meal we talked about mum, laughed, posed for shameless selfies wearing Santa hats my husband brought, and focused on the arrival of baby Mason. His due date was weeks away. We speculated about what he would look like and spent time going through all of the adorable baby stuff my sister had waiting for him at her home. A baby was exactly what our family needed.

My Christmas gift to the family was a video montage of hundreds of photos of Wanda set to awesome music. I had hired someone to add short snippets of her legacy video so we could hear her talking. These moments were sprinkled around the photos. I emailed Team Wanda the video link so mum's voice is always a click away.

We kicked off Christmas morning at my sister Tahlia's for breakfast. Later that day we stopped at my sister Elizabeth's for dinner. This may seem odd given our bereavement but Christmas was pretty close to perfect. No tears, just quality time with our family. The day after Christmas, I spent a few hours at my office. Waiting in a pile of mail was a letter and plaque from St. Jude Children's Research Hospital thanking us for our year of service. This token of appreciation came at the perfect time.

On New Year's Eve we hosted our annual comedy show at the theatre. A big Boston comic was our headliner. A sold out crowd laughed for hours, while I felt a bit lost. The idea of beginning a new year without mum seemed surprisingly strange. We had already crossed so many "firsts" off of our list and yet the first New Year's Eve left a sting that took days to heal. I only include these moments of sorrow to help anyone in this position to realize that in grief there is no time, rhyme or reason.

One minute you can feel happy and proud of the progress you have made in your recovery and the next minute you may find yourself crying in the grocery story standing in front of your loved one's favorite brand of coffee. The important thing is to allow yourself to feel every emotion and to be present in the moment.

Admittedly, I use work as a distraction from grief. I returned to my office the day after my step-son died and the day after mum died. For months, I stayed unbelievably busy. I did it, but I know work doesn't cure grief. I think it is important to note that each time I had real breakthroughs in my grief, real moments of reflection, I was away from work. I found deep levels of healing in the quiet space in my home and my Jeep.

Looking back, I wonder if slowing down a bit more would have helped me process the enormity of my life shift. Wanda always said Americans work too hard. In Italy, shops, museums, and businesses shut down midday for a riposo. The lessons Wanda taught us continue to echo through my head. I can still hear her saying, "Do you know everything closes in Italy after lunch? Europeans recognize the importance of siesta and vacations, naps and recharging." In the spirit of her words of wisdom, I invite you to allow yourself to slow down a bit. Mother always knows best.

Wanda Stairs Howard October 19, 2013

If ever something were true about me, this is it.
"I have learned to give, not because I have too
much, but because I have known the feeling
of not having." ~ Anonymous

43

Playtime is Important

On January 9, 2015, my niece Paige went into labor. At long last we were going to meet baby Mason. Our little prince was coming to infuse magic and joy back into our lives. Mum was on my mind all day. "He's coming," I said out loud in my quiet house. "Today is the day, mum." I believe Wanda had met Mason in heaven the moment she crossed over. He was handpicked and extra special.

I called to see if Paige had any requests while she was busy trying to move a tiny person out of her tiny body. In the background I heard her say, "Chocolate-covered strawberries." Off I went to the closest Edible Arrangements shop.

The ritual of feasting on fruit dipped in chocolate was sort of spiritual for our foodie mother. She loved fresh fruit and chocolate. Near the end of her illness we would stop at Edible Arrangements to purchase a box of chocolate-covered apples and strawberries. We'd eat them in the car. I stocked wet naps in my glovebox for this type of sport.

The song "Happy" came on the radio as it was my turn at the cash register. I began singing as the cashier filled the congratulations balloon. In honor of Wanda, I ordered four pieces of dipped fruit for myself to eat in the car. Just then I received a text from my sister Elizabeth saying Paige was pushing and had begun hard labor.

The small box of fruit, basket for Paige, balloon, and my oversized pocketbook were a lot to balance as I walked out of the shop. I placed my pocketbook on the front passenger seat of my Jeep so I could use two hands to carefully place the fruit basket on the floor in the back. As I situated the basket I heard Wanda's voice talking in the Jeep.

The sound was a little muffled, but she was undeniably speaking to me. Completely astounded, I loudly said, "Mum?! I hear you mum! I can hear you!" From there I began freaking out a bit as her voice continued to fill the car. "Okay, okay, okay...I know you are here, mum. This is Mason's big day. Of course you are here." Just then I stopped talking and listened more closely to her voice.

What I heard then was the tail end of a very long voicemail she had left me ten months prior. I rushed to the front seat and pulled my cell out of my pocketbook. My phone was lit up, playing her voicemail on speakerphone.

To fully grasp the enormity of this heavenly stunt I need to provide some back story. Shortly after Wanda returned to heaven I needed to upgrade my phone. My main concern was saving her text and cell messages. I had to email all of the voicemails to my home computer. From there I had to save the files and download an audio file of her voicemails.

To hear these messages, I have to swipe my phone screen and navigate my way through the apps. This involves four additional swipes. After this, I have to hit the play button. Over ten steps must be taken in order to hear this voicemail from mum. How on earth did this happen in my pocketbook? Not to mention the additional button that needed to be pressed in order for the message to be on speakerphone.

This was by far the most amazing sign Wanda had ever sent. Immediately after the voicemail ended I began sobbing. After I had a good cry, I began laughing, and talking to her. "You are AWESOME, MUM. Awesome! You are so strong. I love you!"

I called my sister Elizabeth who was in the delivery room with Paige. She wasn't the least bit surprised by my story. My sister said, "Of course she is going to send us signs today. She wouldn't miss this for the world." She added that the lights in the delivery room had been flickering for a few hours. They knew mum was with them. Elizabeth decided to play saved voicemails of mum on speakerphone in the hospital room so Mason could hear her voice.

Mason was born with a beautiful balance of both his mother and father. Team Wanda sees a lot of Wanda in Mason. His big toe is the same shape as Wanda's big toe. Mason has a deep dimple in his smile. Wanda had the same dimple. She had placed her trademark on her perfect great-grandson. What better physical gene to inherit? Every time Mason smiles we will see his dimple and remember our happy mother.

Less than a month later we celebrated my nephew Tyler's birthday. His special day fell on Super Bowl Sunday. I hosted a large brunch for our crew. Tyler was the last of the four grandchildren to have a first birthday without Grandma Wanda. I was relieved to have crossed this finish line.

The following week we celebrated my birthday. I smiled and stayed busy throughout the day poking through nurseries with my friend Mo. I wore the heart-shaped MOM locket mum gifted me the year prior. That night Roger took our family out to dinner. I was anxious for the meal (and the day) to end.

This was my first birthday in ten years that mum and I hadn't traveled to our favorite spa at Wentworth by the Sea. I missed her physical body. I missed the two of us lounging on our hotel beds talking about life as we scrolled through our iPads. I missed the sound of her gorgeous voice singing Happy Birthday.

A week later I returned to Wentworth by the Sea for the first time since mum had returned to heaven. Mum's grandkids were excited to revisit their happy place. Their bathing suits were packed the second I announced the getaway. Shortly after mum's passing I wrote to the general manager of Wentworth to let him know how much she treasured her time at Wentworth.

Since our last visit the hotel had finished a facelift renovation. The lobby, dining area, and bar were completely redecorated. I saw this as a metaphorical nod from Wanda. The layout of the rooms is the same, but the color, style, and texture is different. Nothing is ever the same after change. We must find a way to hold on to what we once loved as we adjust to the new view.

Our time at Wentworth was a much-needed break from the unending snowstorms that started shortly after my birthday. Massachusetts had an unprecedented amount of snowfall that winter. The 2015 snow totals broke records in our state. As everyone around me complained about the snow I was grateful for two things: the fabulous snow tubes Roger ordered from L.L. Bean and the extra time I had to stay home and relax. I devoured entire seasons of the shows Homeland and Breaking Bad during the blizzards.

Our house became a sledding and snow tubing lodge. Boots, mittens, hats, snow pants, jackets, and scarves covered the old steam radiators in our home. Rog took pride in the trails he made with my sisters and the kids. They spent hours outside flying down the slopes of our yard while I prepared meals in the kitchen. Some days, baby Mason was my sous chef, seated in his carrier on my kitchen table.

Hot soup, cocoa, and sandwiches were served all day. We even had an outdoor Shirley Temple drink station. The sledding/tubing crew used snow piles as cup holders. We rolled deep with an average of six to fourteen people sledding.

Months after the loss we would send "checking in" text messages to our team. This was our method of reporting who was having a hard day. The person who reported having the blues, would usually receive a follow up text that read something along the lines of:

- I am in the driveway. We are going to for ice cream. Come outside.
- I have candle coupons. Get ready to shop.
- Half price pizza tonight at 6 p.m.
- Manicures tonight at 5 p.m.
- .50 cent wings tonight at 7 p.m. Be ready at 6:45 p.m.

During the sledding/tubing parties, no one was ever blue. Through the kitchen windows I could hear everyone outside laughing and cheering for one another. In these pure moments, surrounded by nature, family, food, and quality sledding and tubing gear, we were *all* happy.

Wanda always took us to parks and the beach when we were little. Years later, she took the grandchildren to the Cape Cod Canal to ride their scooters and bikes. She recognized the importance of being active outside. When schools stopped providing outdoor recess to junior high and middle school students she was outraged. She knew the value of time spent in the fresh air.

I thought of mum as I listened to our silly, sledding, belly-laughing crew. Hearing Team Wanda laugh again was like listening to hope budding beneath the snow.

<u>Wanda Stairs Howard</u> <u>December 31, 2013</u>

If you make friends with yourself, you will
never be alone. - Maxwell Maltz

44

Take Children to the Zoo

FAT TUESDAY HAS ALWAYS BEEN A fabulous day for us. Mardi Gras is the traditional name for the day before Ash Wednesday which is the first day of Lent. Historically this is the day to eat yummy food before the ritual fasting of the Lenten season. Wanda and I always picked up fresh malasadas from a local Portuguese bakery and after we ate one in the Jeep we would drive around to deliver the goods.

This was the first year I was going to pick up the sweet treats without her. When I called the bakery to place the order the woman on the other end of the phone asked my name. "Lorna," I said. The woman tried to confirm the order by repeating my name. "Wanda?" she asked. "No. Lorna. My name is Lorna." Turns out my mother Wanda was going with me to pick up the malasadas. I saw this as another sign. I know that some of you may think I am crazy. Moments like this may be coincidences, but they happened. I find comfort in these coincidences.

It took a while for me to be able to shop in the local places we frequented when Wanda was alive. All of the joy from our epic impulse purchases was replaced with the absence of her. I missed hands placing trinkets into the carriage. The girls at Bath and Body cried when they learned of her death. One store manager, Alice, hugged me and said Wanda touched her heart and inspired her. Whenever I shop at this store the girls still mention mum.

The Ghost Sign UK Facebook group posted a beautiful farewell message to Wanda on their wall. She loved driving around in search of old buildings with ghost signs. She must have been heavenly tickled pink when they posted. In these moments I am reminded of the impact made even on people far away whom she had never met.

For almost fifteen years I have worked part-time at the biggest casting company in Boston. The first winter without mum I was fortunate enough to work on a big movie that was being filmed in Boston. This was a Hollywood A-list project.

As I spoke with one of the most adored actors in America (who just happens to be Wanda's favorite male Italian actor) I couldn't help but think about mum. She would have gone bananas over this story. That night I sent her a text. "I met your favorite actor today. He is one of the kindest people I have ever met. So handsome. I wish we could talk about today. Love you."

I have never been star struck. I see actors as people. The only difference between celebrity actors and most of the fine, hardworking actors I know is fate. This wasn't the case for mum. Whenever she met anyone famous she became a ten-year-old girl seeing the Beatles for the first time.

Whether the person was a radio personality, news anchor, TV personality, Academy Award winning actor, celebrity chef, or high ranking politician, when in their company Wanda always struggled to disguise her excitement. She used to say, "Why should people act like they aren't star struck when they meet celebrities? Wouldn't a lack of enthusiasm be insulting? I mean, shouldn't people be real?"

The movie project brought me to the Italian North End of Boston a lot. I drove down Hanover Street and Commercial Street almost every day. Long before she was born, Wanda's grandfather owned Gandolfo Olive Oil and Produce on Commercial Street. She was extremely proud of her Sicilian heritage. To her the North End was the epitome of her roots. There was something soothing about spending the first winter without mum in one of her favorite places. During my time in the North End I felt less alone.

On my final night of the movie project I sat in a window seat at Carmelina's, my favorite spot in the North End. It was Patriot's Day weekend in Boston and the narrow streets of this historic section of the city were packed. While eating the best eggplant dish this side of Italy I couldn't help but think about mum. Just then a Paul Revere reenactor rode down Hanover Street on a white horse. This is an annual ritual, but the timing could not have been more perfect. *Are you seeing this mum? How much do we love a night in the North End?*

At long last the snow melted and tiny shoots of green began to surface from the dirt. Spring was in the air. Another new season without mum was upon us. In the blink of an eye, the first Easter without Wanda was at our door. I always host Easter. Because of the busy movie schedule, my sister offered to host. Breaking tradition was a perfect way to approach the holiday. That morning the woman behind the bakery counter cried when she realized Wanda was in heaven. She was yet another person who was touched by mum.

This was our first April vacation without Wanda. In her honor we planned daily adventures with the kids. The high point of the week was a trip to the Franklin Park Zoo in Boston. Mum loved the zoo and got a kick out of taking children to see animals. As the kids spoke about past zoo visits with gram and Joey the monkey, it was evident they hadn't forgotten a second of that time with mum. Wanda was smart to invest her time in educational daytrips.

On May 6th, Liz and I packed my Jeep with a hydrangea shrub and headed toward Truro. We wanted to commemorate the day of the miracle that took place a year prior. Leaving a beautiful plant and a letter on the steps at Ava's house felt like the right thing to do. It seemed hard to believe a year had passed since we came to understand the meaning of the buoy projects.

As we approached the picturesque cottage on the sea I felt a moment of nervousness flash through my body. "What if she thinks we are crazy?" I asked my sister." She won't," she replied. Just then I remembered Wanda's advice about being real. If she were alive, she would have been delivering the plant. Nerves and all, Wanda would have boldly knocked on the door. In matters such as this, she was fearless.

As we approached the door I noticed buoys and strands of lights hanging in a tree in the front yard and there were smaller buoys in the window boxes on the house. My heart fluttered as we walked toward the door. The enormity of the meeting a year prior filled my body with electricity.

I could hear the ocean waves in the backyard, birds talking in the trees, and water running through a hose in one of the gardens. The property was filled with peace. A tall, lean man wearing his hair in a ponytail came out of the house. His face had a welcoming smile as he walked toward us. As I began to explain the nature of our visit he stopped me by saying, "Of course. I know who you are. Yes, we remember that day. Ava is out of town today, but I will photograph this lovely gift and send her a picture. Thank you so much."

Liz and I thanked him and made our way back to the Jeep. We drove up the street and parked outside of mum's favorite cottage. We walked around and took a selfie near the door of the cottage. Liz bears an uncanny resemblance to Wanda in the photo. As we sat in the Jeep processing our encounter at Ava's my phone alerted me to a Facebook post.

A woman from our community wrote a comment on my page about the importance of family. She mentioned how lucky we were to have experienced such togetherness during Wanda's illness. Her comment was in response to a thread regarding a post on my wall dated June 1, 2014, the day mum died.

This means the woman had to have gone through nearly a year of Facebook posts on my page to read that message. No one had commented on that thread since June 2, 2014. Was this a wink from Wanda in heaven or another coincidence?

Miraculous things seem to happen every time we are in Truro. Wanda always said there was something magical about the ocean on that part of the Cape. Each time I check the mailbox I hope to find a note from Ava. In the few pieces of correspondence I have sent her, I have included our contact information. Perhaps we were merely facilitators in

God's plan? Perhaps we were never meant to form a relationship beyond the buoy projects.

Wanda Stairs Howard May 18, 2014 · Instagram ·

The Terns eggs are hatching. You can hear them chirping in the dunes. #natureisawesome

45

Encourage Independence

WO DAYS AFTER WE DELIVERED THE hydrangea to Ava's house we celebrated my sister Elizabeth's birthday. She was the last of Team Wanda to blow out the candles on a cake without mum by her side. I stuck to her like glue that week. Liz had just recovered from a serious case of pneumonia.

This particular week, we had three big firsts in a row: May 6th the day of the miracle meeting with Ava, May 8th Liz's birthday, and May 10th Mother's Day. Moments before midnight on Liz's birthday, we saw a shooting star. It is important to note that we weren't lying in a field on a blanket hoping to see shooting stars. We were in the middle of a rare, late night run to Walmart. We both caught the shooting star as it soared from one end of my windshield to the other. It was an awesome, heavenly gift.

On Mother's Day we gathered at mum's house. Doug worked hard cleaning up the yard and hosted a cookout. It was fantastic to see all of mum's plants and flowers in bloom. He honored mum and the buoy projects by displaying a small buoy motif near their shed. He hung mum's netting, arranged a few lobster pots, and re-hung what was left of the enormous buoy collection. It was an absolutely perfect tribute to Wanda on Mother's Day.

All of us contributed to the meal. I brought malasadas and mum's macaroni salad made with elbow macaroni, cucumber, tuna, and mayo. For as long as I can remember, this salad has been a hit at our parties. Mum mixes the mayo with sugar, salt, pepper, and vinegar before adding the rest of the ingredients. The family played badminton in the sunshine, ate oversized portions of food, and relaxed on the deck. It was the type of day that would have made Wanda very happy.

That weekend Doug told me that he had been smelling mum's perfume in the kitchen near the sink. He wondered what message she was trying to send. One day his knees began to bother him while he tended to the yard and gardens. He said that night he went into the cellar and mum's gardening knee pad was in the middle of the floor. These experiences comforted him.

The following week we went to Fenway Park. The day started cold and rainy. When contemplating whether or not to cancel the trip my sister said, "It will all work out. Mum always loved the rain. We will dress in layers. The kids will have fun even if the sun isn't shining."

She was right. The kids had a blast. We hit very little traffic and parked in the front row of the lot, which was less than twenty feet from our ticket gate. As first timers at Fenway the children were treated like royalty. There were given big buttons that read "First Time at Fenway" and little packets of dirt from the field, as well as wristbands. We stopped at the souvenir shop and dressed them in Red Sox T-shirts. They took endless selfies and ate their first Fenway Frank.

The minute we sat in our seats, the sun came out. Just before the first pitch my nephew Trey and niece Taylor asked if they could sit in empty seats in the front row of our section of the ballpark. Our seats were many rows away from the front row.

Wanda always spoke about the importance of children becoming independent. She encouraged parents to allow their children to color and paint on the walls of their bedroom and order their own meals at restaurants and make their own fashion decisions when shopping for clothing. The chance to sit in the season ticket holders empty, front row seats was an unforgettable opportunity for the kids.

Wanda had left her mark on her grandchildren. They were independent free-thinkers who weren't afraid to take risks, color outside of the lines, and think outside of the box. Mum would have said yes, so we said yes. If approached by the folks who purchased the tickets, we told the kids to be polite, say thank you, and head back up to our sitting area. The kids were smiling from ear-to-ear. It was hard to tell if they were more excited about sitting in the front row or sitting away from the grownups who drove them to the game. Within a half hour we received a text message from them asking for snack money.

We couldn't help but laugh each time we saw a vendor walk over to hand them popcorn, cotton candy, pizza, or drinks. At ages ten and thirteen they were making their own change and making the most of their platinum seats at Fenway. About an hour into the game, my niece Taylor sent a text saying she needed to use the restroom. Liz and I walked down to their section so she could bring Taylor to the ladies room.

I was the seat filler in her absence. The view of the park is so much different when seated in the front row. I couldn't help but get caught up in the camaraderie and excitement in the air. My nephew Trey was the happiest I had seen him in months. With his Italian ice seated in the cup holder on the wall of Fenway Park he leaned back in his seat taking it all in. "This is pretty amazing, huh, buddy," I said. "Yes. It's pretty awesome," he replied. The rain stopping, the perfect parking, and the front row seats for the kids; I could not help but take a moment to say thanks to mum. *I am pretty sure you had something to do with tonight. Thanks.*

Just then a player on the other team hit a ball that soared straight toward us. "Oh my gosh, oh my gosh, oh my gosh," I screamed as the ball flew through the air. "Trey, do you see this?" Just then one of the Red Sox players ran over to our section. He and the ball were literally one foot away from Trey, on the field on the other side of the wall. It was thrilling. Less than five minutes later my friend posted a picture of me and Trey at the game on TV. She photographed us on her TV screen. The night was a perfect 10.

Memorial Day was the following weekend. This had been her last day talking, texting, laughing, eating, and drinking coffee on her deck as our mother. The day after, the pain crisis that led to the medically-induced coma happened. I was completely unprepared for the pain and sadness I felt the morning of Memorial Day. Still on a high from our night at Fenway, I never slowed down enough to consider how Memorial Day would feel.

For over ten years I have helped the local veterans organizations find singers for their annual Memorial Day ceremony. After the event I joined Team Wanda at mum's home in Buzzards Bay. Doug was hosting another cookout. Our team was somber. In a flash, a year had passed. We now had to use phrases such as "my mother died last year" rather than "I recently lost my mother." Would this twelve-month milestone in some way minimize our license to mourn? Would this one-year marker mark the end of the socially acceptable period of time in which people who have suffered loss are permitted to show their grief? Only time would tell.

I read a Facebook message a woman named Anne sent a few weeks prior. Anne, a licensed nurse's aide and hospice worker, followed the daily posts about Wanda during the final phase of her life. Although I have never met Anne we share common friends.

In her note she shared how moved she was by the documentation and daily posts about the end of our mother's life. She was so inspired, she found herself using *the same exact words* of the language we used in the bedroom during Wanda's last night on earth. What makes this even more special is that Anne used the words we used to help Wanda cross over while she helped her own mother transition to heaven. She said, "You've got this and we've got you" just before her mother died.

This was the moment I realized the true power of Wanda's decision to share every detail of her life as she prepared to die. She didn't want the act of dying to be swept under a rug. She wanted people to talk about it. Wanda wanted people to think differently about death. Anne's note was proof that she succeeded. She changed the way people approach death and dying.

After Wanda's death, I found myself back at the funeral home to sing at a memorial service for a family friend. I had a stirringly candid moment with a member of the funeral home staff. He said that to date he had never experienced a death march or celebration when removing a deceased person from her home. He said the parade Team Wanda threw is something he will never forget. He was smiling while recounting the stroll through the driveway. "Yes," he said, "we hadn't ever seen anything like that. It was pretty cool."

<u>Wanda Stairs Howard</u> <u>January 27, 2014</u>

One word.... Happy

46

Little Moments are Big Moments

M<small>Y SPIRITS WERE LIFTED ON THE</small> morning of May 29th when mum came to me in a dream. This was only my third dream of her since she died nearly a year prior. In this dream she was standing in the wings backstage in a huge theatre waiting to go on stage. Her hair was perfectly styled. When I saw her I said, "Hey! Where have you been?" (Meaning, where have you been for a year.) She responded with a more recent explanation of her absence by saying, "napping." Then she pointed to her epic hair and said, "can you believe it?!" It was as if she was saying she had slept on her hair and it was still performance ready. Wanda always loved a good hair day.

June 1, the anniversary of Wanda's transition, was our last first to finish. On that morning I received a text message from my sister that read, "I love you." I spent a lot of quiet hours at home posting collages of photos representing every decade of Wanda's life. I enjoyed reading messages from everyone whose life was touched by Wanda.

Although we hadn't planned a way to commemorate the one-year anniversary, there was no way we were going to downplay it. Go big or go home has always been our style. After a series of group text messages, we decided to purchase Chinese sky lanterns. The biodegradable paper lanterns have become extremely popular at weddings and memorial services. During our first stay at Truro, Wanda watched a neighboring family ignite lanterns. Once they floated into the sky she clapped. "Aren't they beautiful?" she said as they floated by.

Lanterns that float toward heaven...could there have been a more perfect way honor the day Wanda returned home? I spent hours on the phone trying to find a local store that carried the lanterns. After several discouraging calls I took to Facebook to ask for suggestions. Within minutes the name of a local hardware store was posted on my wall.

Each of the grandchildren was given a lantern that read "In Memory Of" and the package had a special marker to add handwritten messages. My sisters and I had solid white lanterns that released sparklers out of the bottom as they floated away. Doug had a lantern that read "I love you." Linda was given a purple lantern. For most of Wanda's life purple was her favorite color.

The store with the lanterns is on a lake. When we pulled out of the parking lot my sister spotted two adult swans swimming with their cygnets. Naturally, we stopped the Jeep and took photos of the swan mother with her children. It was a perfect day to stumble upon such a sweet family sighting.

We had lunch that afternoon with baby Mason. It is difficult to feel gloomy when in the company of a beautiful, happy baby. Although Mason brightened our day, gloom was lurking over us in the gray sky. I was fairly certain the lanterns would not rise in the rain.

That night we met at mum's house in Buzzards Bay for pizza. I wore mum's sea glass earrings. Tyler wore her sweatshirt. My sister made purple frosted cupcakes. There were little glimpses of Wanda everywhere. As dinner was ending the sky opened up and water poured from the clouds. "Let's take a vote," Elizabeth said. "Do we try at least one lantern or do we hold off for nicer weather." Team Wanda voted to try at least one lantern.

We drove our vehicles in convoy toward the Cape Cod Canal. For years, mum walked the length of the canal with the grandchildren. This is where Wanda brought the kids to watch the train bridge rise and lower in order to race over the tracks. The canal is where Wanda and the kids watched the ducks dip their heads into the water while exposing their butts. Her pet name for these ducks was Up and Downs. This is where we raced to watch the replica of the Mayflower ship (modeled after the ship the pilgrims sailed to America on) pass through the canal a year before. This is where Wanda was happy.

The team gathered in a small circle and devised a plan for the lighting of the lantern. My nephew Tyler held the lantern with his friends Jenna and Chris as my husband tried to light the flame. While all of this was happening the rest of the team stood close together to serve as a wind barrier.

A man with a dog insisted on joining our group. He inserted senseless chatter whenever he could sneak in a sentence. He had been drinking. It was clear he'd had a rough life; his wrinkled skin resembled cracked leather when he smiled. This was the kind of man Wanda would have offered a cigarette or a kind word. This was the kind of person she never wanted us to overlook. I tried to remember this remarkable quality about Wanda as I became increasingly annoyed by his presence during our special ceremony.

When I explained the sentiment behind our lantern the stranger expressed his condolences. Despite his concern he didn't back away from our group. My cousin Jon's fiancée Karen said, "He is the type of person Auntie Wanda would have befriended. I bet he is somehow with us because of her." Perhaps Wanda was reminding us to be patient and kind to our fellow man.

At long last, the charcoal inside of the lantern ignited and began to fill with hot air. As Team Wanda began to cheer, the lantern rose up a bit and then fell to the ground. The paper of the lantern was becoming soaked by rain. As my nephew Tyler tried and tried to regain the momentum of the lantern, we encouraged him to stomp out the flame. The June 1st ceremony of lanterns was not meant to be.

"Let's take a family picture," I said, insisting that we at least capture our attempt to honor mum. Freezing in our water-stained outfits, we clumped together. The strange man offered to take a picture of all of us. As he counted down he said, "One, two, three. Say spaghetti!" We all repeated "spaghetti" as the stranger snapped a pretty awesome picture of us.

The failed lantern ceremony was a chapter out of Wanda's life lesson playbook. Life isn't perfect. No matter how hard we try we cannot control that which is out of our hands. The only thing we can control is the way in which we handle the situation. In this moment what mattered the most is that we were all together. Laughing and supporting one another, we were working toward a healing goal.

In the eyes of Wanda, the end result was far less important than the journey. "Celebrate every little moment," she'd say, "Because in the end you'll realize that all of the little moments were pretty big." We made a plan to release the rest of the lanterns in July on her 61st birthday, unless, of course, it rains. Wanda always did love the rain.

Wanda Stairs Howard October 14, 2011

In April of 2009 I was diagnosed with Stage 3 Invasive Breast Cancer.
The words no one wants to hear, but after
the initial shock, I am here to tell
anyone who's newly diagnosed that you can
get through this and you can survive.
I learned many things during my journey and
when asked what helped me the most
I have to say 3 things,
1st: HUMOR can make anything easier- don't be afraid to laugh...it's
empowering!
2nd: TENACITY Just move one foot in front of
the other. It sounds clichéd but it's true.
When you've faced four surgeries, 16 weeks
of chemotherapy and 33 days of
radiation, you can't look at the long road or the big picture. Just one
step at a time. Counting down after each one helped, too. Like "2
down so many to go!" Each session felt like a victory when I was done.
3rd: FAMILY you have no idea how much
you need them and love them. I
couldn't have gotten through it without them.

October is Breast Cancer month but it is also on Oct 14, 2009 that I finished my chemotherapy. This is what I looked like 2 years ago today. Allow me to borrow this anonymous quote:

YOU NEVER KNOW HOW STRONG YOU ARE
UNTIL STRENGTH IS YOUR ONLY OPTION.

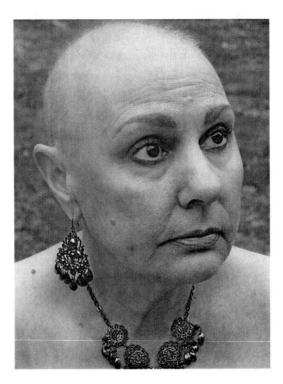

Wanda in 2009 after she completed chemotherapy.

Afterword

I HEARD FROM OUR FRIEND DOUG. HE and his husband Jack had just returned from a vacation in Provincetown, Massachusetts. Provincetown is at the tip of Cape Cod, touching the town of Truro. Some years prior, Doug had injured his foot and as a result, he occasionally walked with a cane. On Memorial Day 2015, Doug and Jack were walking with their dogs on the beach when Doug noticed a large buoy in a pile of driftwood in the sand.

Remembering Wanda's love of buoys and this particular section of Cape Cod he considered this a hello from heaven. Once he picked up the buoy he realized it was attached to a long stick. The buoy served as a perfect walking stick for the beach. I remember liking the pictures the weekend Doug posted them to his Facebook page.

The real surprise came weeks later. While looking at the walking stick buoy Doug had placed in his backyard he noticed undeniable angel evidence. The markings on the side of the buoy read: P. MASON. Wanda's first grandchild Paige is Mason's mother. P. MASON. Remember to look for the signs. They are all around us.

Last week, I rested under the blankets in our bed looking up at the ceiling. It was around 6:00 a.m. and the morning sunlight was filling the room. Mum was on my mind. I hadn't put in my contact lenses. With blurred vision, I looked up from our bed and noticed the ceiling fan. The five points of the brown fan resembled a starfish. I have glanced at this fan for over eighteen years and have only ever seen brown blades. Now all I see is a starfish. I begin and end every day glancing up and smiling with thoughts of mum.

The credit cards that funded our bucket listing are paid off. It took almost a year to accumulate the debt and almost a year to erase it. Every time I made a payment I was reminded of our most awesome adventures. I can still hear mum cheering, "Look at my hair" on Newbury Street. I see her dangling her feet in her new Teiks shoes while seated in a chair on her deck. Together we built memories. No matter how expensive or affordable the adventure, we were blessed to have the extra time together.

I cannot for one moment regret going into debt during that period of time. Although not everyone is in a position to exhaust credit cards, I knew I could find extra work to pay them off as quickly as I maxed them out. This was a choice that was right for me.

My theatre company celebrated its twentieth anniversary in business the summer after Wanda died. We commemorated two decades with a faculty and alumni production of Gypsy. On opening night, the father of the woman playing Mama Rose went across the street to buy a cold soda before the show started.

As he stood in our office drinking a Coke, he said, "Hey, it looks like your mother came to opening night. She must be celebrating your twentieth with us." The name Wanda was written on the label of the bottle of Coke. He realized this as he was standing next to a framed picture of Wanda hanging in the lobby.

Mason's development marks the passage of time. I see Wanda's sparkle in his eyes. I feel her love in his hugs. I hear her happiness in his laughter. I remember her humor when I see his dimple. I think of our time together at the beach when I kiss his big toe. We feel an immeasurable amount of gratitude. We are thankful for Wanda and all that she taught us. Above all, we are grateful for her love.

Photographer for Lorna J. Brunelle: Kim Kennedy

Hair and makeup artist for Lorna J. Brunelle: Mariolga Pantazopoulos

Lorna J. Brunelle is a graduate of The Boston Conservatory. In 2010, she released the Amazon bestseller *Dirty Bombshell - From Thyroid Cancer Back to Fabulous*. A cancer survivor, Lorna has collaborated with The Massachusetts Eye and Ear Infirmary, and has been featured in several publications and documentaries. She is a recipient of the Massachusetts General Hospital "the one hundred" award for her effort to eradicate cancer. The Boston City Council proclaimed October 22 as Lorna J. Brunelle Day for her tireless work in the cancer community. Lorna has been a patient advocate for many years and dedicates her time to a number of organizations. She owns The Burt Wood School of Performing Arts and The Alley Theatre and works at Boston Casting Inc. Lorna resides with her husband Roger in Massachusetts.

Twitter: @LornaBrunelle

Instagram: @Lornabrunelle

Website: www.thebuoyprojects.com

Facebook: The Buoys Projects - A Story of Breast Cancer, Bucket-Lists, Life Lessons, Facebook and Love

Email: info@thebuoyprojects.com

Wanda's father Raymond Stairs holding her in 1954.
Wanda's aunt June is proudly standing by.

Wanda the bright eyed baby.

Wanda as a toddler modeling a bonnet.

Wanda showing her dance moves.

This was one of Wanda's favorite outfits. She loved
this 1960's picture showcasing her teenage style.

Wanda always had great hair, especially in the 60's.

Wanda embracing her 1970's groove.

Long hair, jeans and freshly painted toes. Wanda loved to be barefoot.

Wanda the fashion plate in the 70's in Watertown, Massachusetts.

Gold chain with her Italian hand and horn (to ward off the evil eye or malocchio), gold hoop earrings, and naturally curly hair, this is classic Wanda in the 1980's.

Wanda was a beauty with bangs in the 1980's.

Wanda dancing with her father Ray in the 90's.

Her unforgettable smile.

Wanda in the early 90's.

Tahlia's favorite photo of Wanda.

Doug and Wanda in Rockport, Massachusetts.

Wanda and Doug at the beach.

One of Doug's favorite photos of Wanda.

Tahlia and Wanda on Tal's 21st birthday.

Wanda, Doug and Tahlia one Christmas in the 90's.

Wanda with Elizabeth on Liz's wedding day October 19, 2002.

Wanda graduating from the Kinyon - Campbell
Business School seen here with Lorna.

Wanda with her granddaughter Paige and
grandson Tyler on the Cape Cod Canal.

Wanda with all four of her grandchildren Paige, Tyler, Taylor and Trey at Old Silver Beach on Cape Cod July of 2009.

Wanda with her grandson Tyler the summer of 2013.

Wanda with her grandson Trey the summer of 2013.

Wanda with her granddaughter Taylor.

Wanda with her granddaughter Paige.

Wanda with Paige in Salem, Massachusetts the summer of 2013.

One of Elizabeth's favorite photos with Wanda holding bags of shells at Good Harbor Beach in Gloucester, Massachusetts in October 2013.

Wanda with Linda on Wanda's deck the summer of 2013.

Wanda with her nephew Jon.

Wanda with her dog Emma Mae.

Lorna's favorite photo of Wanda on the beach with Tyler.

One of Wanda's favorite photos on the island
of Cuttyhunk, Massachusetts.

The spirit of Wanda seen here as she dances
near a water fountain in Boston.

Wanda and Lorna sailing in Newport, Rhode
Island with Sailing Heals October 6, 2013.

Team Wanda's favorite photo of Wanda on
Cuttyhunk on October 17, 2013.

Wanda's great-grandson Mason who was born on January 9,
2015. Seven months after Wanda returned to heaven.

Photo credit: Linsey Wakefield Photography

CPSIA information can be obtained at www.ICGtesting.com
Printed in the USA
LVOW11s1117260816

501914LV00006B/88/P